Morocco

To Berthe Abbou and Zhor Hamayed

Ghislaine Bénady and Najat Sefrioui

Photography by Michel Reuss

Morocco

recipes and stories from East Africa

whitecap

kemia and small first courses

Lemons, olives, and argan oil

Preserved lemons and olives are indispensable ingredients in tagines, but they are just as essential as an hors d'oeuvre and can remain on the table as an accompaniment to the courses that follow. In Morocco, preserved lemons are made with very small round fruit but there is nothing to stop you making them with larger, oval-shaped lemons (see page 10). Delicatessens sell all manner of marinated olives mixed with other ingredients but you can also prepare them yourself: simply marinate the olives with chilies, garlic, cilantro, and broiled bell pepper in the refrigerator for a day or so to impart their flavors. Olive oil seasons vegetables and salads and its fruity aroma lifts and enhances the other ingredients. But argan oil adds a more delicate touch, a nutty aroma to a whole range of salads, in particular those using bell peppers (page 20). Tossing couscous grains in it gives a wonderful flavor.

preserved lemons
makes 2 lb (1 kg) · 1 day soaking · 3 weeks maceration

2 lb (1 kg) untreated lemons
3/4 cup (185 mL) coarse salt

Thoroughly wash the lemons before soaking them in cold water for 1 day, changing the water two or three times.

Starting at the tip, make two fairly deep incisions in the form of a cross in each lemon. Open the cut as much as possible and fill with salt. Arrange the filled lemons immediately in one or more preserving jars, packing them tightly and firming them down—it should be difficult to close the lid.

Leave to macerate for 3 weeks.

shrimp cigars
makes 40 · preparation 20 minutes · cooking 20 minutes

2 garlic cloves
1 large bunch of flat-leaf parsley
1 large bunch of cilantro
1 Tbsp (15 mL) sunflower oil
1 lb (500 g) cooked shrimp, deveined
1/2 Tbsp (7.5 mL) mild paprika
1/4 tsp (1 mL) cayenne pepper
2 eggs, beaten
10 sheets of warka or phyllo pastry
egg white for sealing pastries
oil for deep-frying
salt

Peel and crush the garlic and wash and chop the parsley and cilantro. Heat the sunflower oil in a large skillet or pan and fry the shrimp, garlic, and herbs. Season with the spices and cook until the mixture comes away from the pan. Add the eggs and quickly mix in. Remove from the heat and let cool.

Meanwhile, separate the warka or phyllo sheets. Cut each into four squares and fold each square into a triangle. Place some of the filling along the longest edge of each triangle, almost to the ends. Tuck in the ends over the filling then roll up the cigar toward the point. Seal the pastry with a dab of egg white.

Heat the oil and deep-fry the cigars until golden. Drain on paper towels before serving.

fresh salad
serves 6 · preparation 15 minutes

2 tomatoes, peeled
1 small cucumber
1 small green bell pepper
2 salad onions
1 small chili (optional)
2 quarters of preserved lemon, rind only
1 Tbsp (15 mL) vinegar
2 Tbsp (30 mL) olive oil
1/2 tsp (2 mL) ground cumin
1/2 tsp (2 mL) mild paprika
salt and pepper
black olives (unpitted)

Skin the tomatoes and cucumber and remove the seeds from the tomatoes and the bell pepper.

Cut all the vegetables and the lemon into small dice and place in a salad bowl. Dress with the vinegar, oil, spices, and salt and pepper and garnish with a few black olives.

spicy fequas
preparation 15 minutes · cooking 20 minutes · resting 24 hours

1 package active dry yeast
2 lb (1 kg) all-purpose flour
1/2 tsp (2 mL) cayenne pepper
1/2 tsp (2 mL) salt
1 cup (250 mL) shredded Gruyère or other
    semi-hard cheese
2/3 cup (160 mL) oil
2 Tbsp (30 mL) butter, melted

Tip all the ingredients into a large bowl and
mix well. Work with your hands, adding a little
tepid water if necessary, until you have a soft,
pliable dough.

Preheat the oven to 350°F (180°C/Gas 4).

Form the dough into rolls the size of a fat cigar
and place on a greased cookie sheet. Bake for
15 minutes without browning. Let rest for 24 hours.

Preheat the oven to 350°F (180°C/Gas 4).

Cut the rolls into slices 1/4 inch (0.5 cm) thick.
Arrange on a cookie sheet and brown in the
oven for 3 minutes.

meat pastries
makes 12 · preparation 30 minutes · cooking 25 minutes

3 eggs
1 heaping Tbsp (20 mL) butter
7 oz (200 g) ground beef
1 bunch of flat-leaf parsley, snipped
pinch of saffron
1/2 cup (125 mL) shredded semi-hard cheese
1 lb (500 g) puff pastry
salt and pepper

Hard-boil 1 egg, then cool under cold running water.
Meanwhile, melt the butter in a skillet with the
salt and pepper and brown the beef for 5 minutes.
Let cool.

Peel the hard-boiled egg and shred it into a salad
bowl. Add the parsley, saffron, beef, cheese, and
1 raw egg and mix together by hand.

Preheat the oven to 350°F (180°C/Gas 4).

Roll out the pastry and cut into 12 small rounds
with a cookie cutter or using a glass. Place a little
of the filling in the center of each, fold over to
enclose, and brush each one with the third egg,
beaten, to glaze and seal.

Place on a greased cookie sheet and bake
for 15 minutes.

almond bites
preparation 20 minutes · cooking 15 minutes

11/2 cups (375 mL) whole almonds
1 lb (500 g) puff pastry
1 egg yolk

Sprinkle the almonds with salted water and grill for
about 10 minutes in a dry skillet over medium heat,
stirring from time to time.

Preheat the oven to 400°F (200°C/Gas 6).

Remove the pastry from the refrigerator, roll out,
and cut into rounds using a 11/2-inch (4-cm) cookie
cutter. Place an almond in the center of each, fold
over to enclose, and glaze with the egg yolk.

Place on a greased cookie sheet, and bake
for 15 minutes.

savory aniseed cookies
preparation 10 minutes · resting 1 hour · cooking 10 minutes

23/4 cups (685 mL) all-purpose flour
3/4 cup (185 mL) cornstarch
2 eggs, beaten
1/2 cup (125 mL) shredded semi-hard cheese
3/4 cup + 2 Tbsp (215 mL) softened butter
2 Tbsp (30 mL) milk
1 tsp (5 mL) baking powder
1/4 tsp (1 mL) salt
1/4 tsp (1 mL) pepper
1/4 tsp (1 mL) ground aniseed
1/2 tsp (2 mL) sesame seeds
1 egg yolk for glazing

Mix the flour and the cornstarch with the eggs then
add all the remaining ingredients, except the egg
yolk. Work rapidly with your hands without over-
kneading, then let the dough rest in the fridge for
1 hour.

Preheat the oven to 400°F (200°C/Gas 6).

Remove the dough and roll out. Cut out the cookies
with a 1-inch (2.5 cm) cookie cutter. Place them on
a greased cookie sheet and glaze the tops with the
egg yolk. Bake for 10 minutes.

kemia and small first courses

beet and cumin salad
serves 6 • preparation 5 minutes

3 medium beets, cooked
1 garlic clove, peeled and crushed
$1/2$ tsp (2 mL) ground cumin
1 lemon
1 Tbsp (15 mL) olive oil
salt

Peel the beets, cut them into small pieces, and place in a small bowl with salt, to taste, and the garlic and cumin. Drizzle over the lemon juice and oil. Mix together and serve chilled.

eggplant "caviar"
serves 6 • preparation 15 minutes • cooking 15 minutes

2 lb (1 kg) eggplants
2 lb (1 kg) tomatoes
$1/2$ bunch of cilantro
$1/2$ bunch of flat-leaf parsley
$1/2$ tsp (2 mL) ground cumin
$1/2$ tsp (2 mL) paprika
3 garlic cloves, peeled and crushed
$2/3$ cup (160 mL) water
2 Tbsp (30 mL) olive oil
salt
preserved lemon and lemon-marinated olives

Wash the eggplants, tomatoes, cilantro, and parsley. Trim and part-peel the eggplants, leaving strips of the skin intact, then dice the flesh. Peel the tomatoes, squeeze them to release the juice, then dice the flesh. Snip the herbs.

Place the eggplants and tomatoes with the spices in a pressure-cooker and add the herbs, the spices, and the garlic. Add the water and oil, and season with salt. Mix well, close the lid firmly, and cook over gentle heat for 10 minutes then remove the lid and let the "caviar" reduce. If you do not have a pressure cooker, place the ingredients in a heavy-based pot as above, cover, and cook over gentle heat for 30 minutes. Remove the lid and let the "caviar" reduce before serving.

Serve garnished with strips of preserved lemon and lemon-marinated olives.

fava bean salad
serves 6 • preparation 10 minutes • cooking 20 minutes

1 preserved lemon
1 bunch of cilantro
3 Tbsp (45 mL) olive oil
3 garlic cloves, peeled and crushed
$3/4$ cup + 1 Tbsp (200 mL) water
1 Tbsp (15 mL) paprika
2 lb (1 kg) fava beans, freshly shelled, or 1 lb (500 g) frozen beans
salt
preserved lemon and handful of green olives

Soak the preserved lemon in warm water for 5 minutes to remove the salt. Wash the cilantro then snip with scissors.

Put the oil in a large pan with the garlic, salt to taste, and cilantro. Pour in the water and stir to mix well.

Place on the heat and let simmer over low heat for 5 minutes before adding the paprika and the beans. Let cook for 15-20 minutes until the sauce has reduced.

Serve garnished with strips of preserved lemon and the olives.

carrot salad

serves 6 · preparation 15 minutes · cooking 15 minutes

2 lb (1 kg) slender carrots
2 garlic cloves (unpeeled)
3 Tbsp (45 mL) vinegar
1 Tbsp (15 mL) olive oil
$1/2$ tsp (2 mL) ground cumin
$1/2$ tsp (2 mL) paprika
$1/2$ bunch of flat-leaf parsley
pinch of cayenne pepper (optional)
salt

Peel the carrots with a paring knife. Cut into batons and drop into boiling salted water with the garlic. Cook until the carrots are tender then drain and let cool.

Meanwhile, make the dressing. Peel the garlic, scrape the pulp into a bowl, and crush with a fork. Add the vinegar, oil, spices, snipped parsley, and salt to taste. If you like a little heat, add the cayenne too. Gently mix the carrots with the dressing and serve.

zucchini salad

serves 6 · preparation 10 minutes · cooking 10 minutes

2 lb (1 kg) slender zucchini
2 garlic cloves (unpeeled)
3 Tbsp (45 mL) lemon juice
1 Tbsp (15 mL) olive oil
$1/2$ tsp (2 mL) ground cumin
$1/2$ tsp (2 mL) paprika
salt

Wash the zucchini but do not peel. Cut into thick batons and drop into boiling salted water with the garlic. Cook until the zucchini are tender then drain and let cool.

Peel the garlic, scrape the pulp into a bowl, and crush with a fork. Add the lemon juice, oil, spices, and salt to taste, and mix well. Gently mix the zucchini with the dressing and serve.

cauliflower salad

serves 6 · preparation 10 minutes · cooking 15 minutes

1 large cauliflower
2 garlic cloves (unpeeled)
3 Tbsp (45 mL) vinegar
1 Tbsp (15 mL) olive oil
$1/2$ tsp (2 mL) ground cumin
$1/2$ tsp (2 mL) paprika
$1/2$ bunch of flat-leaf parsley
salt

Wash the cauliflower and cut into small florets. Drop into boiling salted water with the garlic. Cook until the florets are tender then drain and let cool.

Peel the garlic, scrape the pulp into a bowl, and crush with a fork. Add the vinegar, oil, spices, the snipped parsley, and salt to taste. Gently mix the cauliflower with the dressing and serve.

broiled bell peppers with argan oil
Serves 6 • preparation 5 minutes • cooking 20 minutes

6 large green bell peppers
3 garlic cloves
1 lemon
1/2 tsp (2 mL) ground cumin
2 Tbsp (30 mL) argan oil
salt

Preheat the broiler and broil the peppers, turning so that they are broiled on all sides. Remove from the heat and put in a polythene bag to cool. Once cool, remove the skins and seeds. Cut the flesh into pieces.

Peel the garlic and cut into tiny pieces. Squeeze the lemon.

Put the peppers in a bowl and mix with the lemon juice, garlic, cumin, oil, and salt to taste. Serve cold.

broiled bell peppers with lemon
serves 6 • preparation 5 minutes • cooking 20 minutes

6 large green bell peppers
3 garlic cloves
1 lemon
1/2 tsp (2 mL) ground cumin
2 Tbsp (30 mL) olive oil
salt

Preheat the broiler and broil the peppers, turning so that they are broiled on all sides. Remove from the heat and put in a polythene bag to cool. Once cool, remove the skins and seeds. Cut the flesh into pieces.

Peel the garlic and cut into tiny pieces. Squeeze the lemon.

Put the peppers in a bowl and mix with the lemon juice, garlic, cumin, oil, and salt to taste. Serve cold.

bell pepper and tomato salad
serves 6 • preparation 10 minutes • cooking 20 minutes

1 lb (500 g) bell peppers
1/2 preserved lemon
2 lb (1 kg) tomatoes
3 Tbsp (45 mL) olive oil
salt

Preheat the broiler and broil the peppers, turning so that they are broiled on all sides. Remove from the heat and put in a polythene bag to cool. Once cool, remove the skins and seeds.

Meanwhile soak the preserved lemon in warm water for 5 minutes to remove the salt. Peel the tomatoes, remove the seeds and juice, and cut the flesh into slices.

Cut the peppers into long slices and add the tomatoes and the preserved lemon, cut into tiny pieces. Dress with the oil and salt to taste.

spicy ratatouille
serves 6 • preparation 15 minutes • cooking 25 minutes

2 lb (1 kg) ripe tomatoes
1 lb (500 g) green bell peppers
1 bunch of flat-leaf parsley
1 bunch of cilantro
3 garlic cloves
1/4 cup (60 mL) olive oil
1/2 tsp (2 mL) ground cumin
1 Tbsp (15 mL) sweet paprika
1/4 tsp (1 mL) hot paprika
3/4 cup + 1 Tbsp (200 mL) water
salt

Wash the tomatoes and the peppers before cutting into pieces. Wash the herbs and peel and finely chop the garlic.

Heat the oil in a large, heavy-based pot, add the tomato and cook for 5 minutes, then add the peppers, herbs, garlic, spices, and salt to taste. Moisten with the water, lower the heat, and let reduce, stirring from time to time with a spatula. Serve warm.

kemia and small first courses

sweet potato and raisin salad
serves 6 • preparation 15 minutes • soaking 5 minutes • cooking 25 minutes

2 lb (1 kg) sweet potatoes
$^2/_3$ cup (160 mL) raisins
1 Tbsp (15 mL) peanut oil
$^1/_4$ cup (60 mL) butter
1 small onion, peeled and finely shredded
$^1/_2$ tsp (2 mL) ground ginger
pinch of saffron
$^3/_4$ cup + 1 Tbsp (200 mL) water
$^1/_2$ tsp (2 mL) cinnamon
1 Tbsp (15 mL) sugar
1 Tbsp (15 mL) honey
pinch of salt and pepper

Try to select orange-fleshed sweet potatoes and brown rather than golden raisins for extra contrast in the presentation.

Peel the sweet potatoes and cut into 1-inch (2-cm) thick rounds or in pieces. Soak the raisins in a bowl of very hot water.

Heat the oil and butter in a large, heavy-based pot and soften the onion over gentle heat. Add the ginger, saffron, salt, and pepper and stir for 5 minutes. Moisten with the water. Once it bubbles, add the sweet potato and cook for 10 minutes. Add the drained raisins, then the cinnamon, sugar, and honey. Lower the heat and let simmer for 10 minutes until you have a thick, rich sauce. Serve warm.

orange and olive salad
serves 6 • preparation 15 minutes • refrigeration 1 hour

3 large oranges
3 garlic cloves
$^1/_2$ tsp (2 mL) chili powder
2 Tbsp (30 mL) olive oil
2 Tbsp (30 mL) lemon juice (about 1 lemon)
1 cup (250 mL) black Greek olives
salt

Peel the oranges, removing all pith and membrane. Cut the segments into pieces and put into a salad bowl. Peel and finely chop the garlic and add to the bowl.

Season with the chili powder, oil, lemon juice, and salt to taste. Gently incorporate the olives.

Chill in the refrigerator for at least 1 hour. Serve cold.

garlic-fried chilies
serves 6 • preparation 15 minutes • cooking 5 minutes

6 green chili peppers
2 garlic cloves
salt
oil for frying

Wash and dry the chilies. Peel and grate the garlic.

Heat a little oil in a skillet and fry the chilies, turning regularly. Transfer to a plate covered with paper towels, then arrange in a shallow dish. Very rapidly brown the garlic in the skillet.

Season the chilies with the garlic and salt, to taste.

soups

harira fassia

serves 6 · preparation 15 minutes · cooking 40 minutes

4 ripe tomatoes
2 onions
1 Tbsp (15 mL) tomato paste
2^1/$_2$ cups (625 mL) water
^{1}/$_2$ cup (125 mL) all-purpose flour
1 Tbsp (15 mL) butter
7 oz (200 g) cubed veal
3^1/$_2$ oz (100 g) cubed lamb
1^1/$_2$ cups (375 mL) canned, drained chickpeas
a few celery leaves
2 bunches of cilantro
1 bunch of flat-leaf parsley
^{1}/$_4$ tsp (1 mL) pepper
1 sachet of saffron colorant or ^{1}/$_4$ tsp turmeric
pinch of powdered saffron
^{1}/$_4$ tsp (1 mL) ground ginger
^{1}/$_2$ cup (125 mL) lentils
^{1}/$_4$ cup (60 mL) short-grain rice
salt

Peel the tomatoes and onions and cut into very small pieces. Blend the tomato paste with half the water and the flour.

Put the butter in a large, heavy-based pot with the tomatoes, onions, veal, lamb, chickpeas, celery leaves, herbs, spices, and salt to taste. Cover with water and cook for 15 minutes, then add the lentils.

Let cook for an additional 10 minutes until everything is cooked through, then add the remaining measured water. As soon as it returns to a boil, add the diluted tomato paste and stir with a spatula for 10 minutes to prevent lumps forming. Add the rice 15 minutes before the end and snip the remaining cilantro over the dish before serving.

soup with couscous and aniseed
serves 6 • preparation 2 minutes • cooking 18 minutes

2 cups (500 mL) water
1/4 cup (60 mL) butter
1/2 tsp (2 mL) turmeric
1/4 tsp (1 mL) pepper
11/3 cups (330 mL) coarse-grain couscous
1 Tbsp (15 mL) ground aniseed
salt

Put the water, butter, turmeric, pepper, and salt to taste in a large saucepan. Bring to a boil then tip in the couscous in a steady stream with half the aniseed. Stir from time to time during cooking.

If the couscous swells too much, add a little extra water and stir to prevent lumps forming. Let simmer for 15 minutes over low heat then add the remaining aniseed. Serve hot.

quick chicken soup
serves 6 • preparation 10 minutes • cooking 30 minutes

3 tomatoes
1 bunch of flat-leaf parsley
1 bunch of cilantro
2 potatoes
1 large onion
5 quarts (5 L) water
8 large chicken wings
1 heaping Tbsp (20 mL) butter
1/4 tsp (1 mL) pepper
1/4 tsp (1 mL) turmeric
1/4 cup (60 mL) rice
salt

Wash the tomatoes and herbs. Peel the potatoes and onion and cut in half. Put the water in a large, heavy-based pot with the chicken wings, tomatoes, potatoes, onion, herbs, pepper, turmeric, and salt to taste and bring to a boil. Cook for 25 minutes.

Remove the herbs. Remove and reserve the chicken wings.

Strain the vegetables, reserving the bouillon, and pass them through a vegetable mill to blend smoothly.

Return the blended vegetables, the bouillon, and the chicken wings to the pot and return to a boil. Add the rice in a steady stream, stir, and cook for an additional 5 minutes. This soup is traditionally served with honey cakes.

vegetable chorba
serves 6 • preparation 20 minutes • cooking 35 minutes

7 oz (200 g) veal or lamb
1 onion
4 carrots
2 leeks
3 potatoes
3 turnips
2 tomatoes
4 cups (1 L) water
1/4 tsp (1 mL) pepper
1/2 tsp (2 mL) turmeric
1 bunch of cilantro
1 bunch of flat-leaf parsley
1/3 cup (80 mL) vermicelli
1 Tbsp (15 mL) tomato paste
1 heaping Tbsp (20 mL) butter
salt

Cut the meat into small cubes and peel and finely slice the onion. Peel all the vegetables and cut into small cubes.

Bring the water to a boil in a large saucepan then add the meat, onion, pepper, turmeric, and salt to taste. Let cook for 20 minutes.

Add all the prepared vegetables. Wash and snip the cilantro and parsley into the pan. Let cook for an additional 12 minutes until the vegetables are cooked, then add the vermicelli and tomato paste and continue to cook for 8 minutes. Stir in the butter just before serving.

tagines

the cooking pot

The tagine, a traditional rustic dish, is a meat (or fish) braise where the flavors mingle with not only the vegetables and spices but also with dried fruits and preserved lemons (see page 8). The magic is performed by the lid of the cooking utensil, a round, glazed terra cotta dish that lends its name to the braise. Shaped like a tall conical chimney, it allows the trapped steam to rise and fall, steaming the ingredients inside. It works on the principle of a braiser, effectively circulating the flavors and aromas. The tagine pot sits on a *"braséro"* or *"qanou,"* which is also made from terra cotta, but it can also be used on top of the stove with a heat-diffusing mat. If you don't possess a tagine, a cast-iron pot or Dutch oven will do the job, for the secret of the dish also lies in cooking it over very low heat for a long time.

meat

Lamb, veal, chicken, duck, quail, and rabbit are the types of meat that lend themselves very well to a tagine. To ensure the meat becomes rich and meltingly tender, select your cuts carefully: too lean and you risk the meat drying out (this applies equally to meatballs). Using meat with a higher fat content means you don't have to add anything extra to the dish. For beef, round, shank, or chuck steak are good choices; shin or leg of veal likewise. Foreshank of lamb is the cut of choice, but shoulder is a less costly option. Ask your butcher to bone and trim the meat then cut it into large pieces. For poultry, use whole farm birds with plump, flavorsome meat, and either cut them yourself or ask the butcher to prepare it for you.

vegetables

Onion, garlic, and fresh herbs are the pillars of Moroccan cuisine but the choice of vegetables and fruit for a tagine is determined by the season. In spring, the first, very tender fava beans are cooked whole; later they are quickly blanched and shelled. From spring to early summer is the season for fresh peas, green beans, zucchini, wild sunchokes, and eggplants. Tomatoes, cucumbers, and bell peppers come into their own in summer and, by fall, it's the time for turnips and quince. Cauliflower, celery, fennel, and pumpkin are the winter vegetables. The vegetables of the day determine the ingredients in a tagine, just like the choice of salads that precede it.

spices

The richness of Moroccan cuisine rests largely on the strongly aromatic flavors of the spices and spice mixes prepared by each cook. For example, ras-el-hanout is a mixture comprising up to thirty different spices: saffron, cumin, coriander, turmeric, ginger, hot chili, paprika, cardamom, cinnamon, but also clove and star anise... If you buy loose spices sold by weight, keep them in small quantities sealed in small jars so that they don't lose their flavor. Saffron, always used in minute quantities, is found in powdered form or in threads.

dried fruits

The use of dried fruits in Moroccan cuisine, giving many recipes their sweet-sour flavor and unique character, is a Persian influence, introduced by the Arabs. Dates, figs, and prunes find their way into dishes and their flesh thickens sauces and flavors the meat.

tagines

chicken with parsley
serves 6 • preparation 15 minutes • cooking 25 minutes

1 large onion
3 garlic cloves
3 Tbsp (45 mL) olive oil
1 whole chicken, weighing about 3 lb (1.5 kg),
   cut into pieces
pinch of saffron
1 cup (250 mL) water
2 large tomatoes
1 bunch of flat-leaf parsley
1 preserved lemon
2 cups (500 mL) green olives, pitted
1/4 tsp (1 mL) pepper
salt

Peel and finely chop the onion and garlic. Heat the
oil in a large, heavy-based pot and soften the onion
and garlic. Season the chicken pieces and add to
the pot, one at a time, to brown on all sides for
5 minutes. Add the saffron and the water, cover
the pot, and let cook over medium heat for
15 minutes.

Skin the tomatoes and cut into small pieces. Wash
and snip the parsley and cut the lemon into fine
strips. Add them all to the pot, lower the heat a
little, and let the sauce reduce slightly. Add the
well-rinsed olives and season with the pepper and
salt, to taste. Serve the chicken with the sauce and
arrange the olives round the sides.

chicken with carrots
serves 6 • preparation 20 minutes • cooking 30 minutes

2 lb (1 kg) carrots
1 large onion
2 large garlic cloves
1 whole chicken, weighing about 3 lb (1.5 kg),
   cut into pieces
2 Tbsp (30 mL) olive oil
pinch of saffron
1/4 tsp (1 mL) turmeric
1/4 tsp (1 mL) ground ginger
1 cup (250 mL) water
1 Tbsp (15 mL) chopped flat-leaf parsley
1 lemon
pinch of pepper
salt

Peel and wash the carrots and cut them into sticks.
Peel and finely chop the onion and crush the
garlic. Season the chicken.

Heat the oil in a large, heavy-based pot and brown
the chicken pieces with the onion, garlic, and
spices. Add the water and let simmer over medium
heat for 10 minutes, then add the carrots and cook
for an additional 15 minutes.

When the sauce has reduced slightly, sprinkle with
the parsley and the lemon juice.

Turn off the heat after 5 minutes and season with
a pinch of pepper and salt, to taste.

chicken with preserved lemon
serves 6 • preparation 15 minutes • cooking 25 minutes

2 large onions
3 garlic cloves
2 Tbsp (30 mL) olive oil
pinch of saffron
1/4 tsp (1 mL) turmeric
1/4 tsp (1 mL) ground ginger
pinch of pepper
2/3 cup (160 mL) water
1 whole chicken, weighing about 3 lb (1.5 kg)
2 preserved lemons
2 cups (500 mL) purple olives
pinch of salt

Peel and slice the onion and cut the garlic into
rounds. Heat the oil in a large, heavy-based pot.
Add the onion and let brown, then add the garlic
and all the spices. Stir and, as soon as the mixture
sizzles, add the water and bring to a boil before
putting in the chicken. Let cook, turning from time
to time, so that it colors on all sides.

Rinse the preserved lemons, cut them in half, and
cut two of the halves, with the pulp, into pieces
and add to the pot. Season and let simmer over
low heat for about 20 minutes.

As soon as the chicken is tender, transfer to a
serving platter and pour the sauce around it. Cut
the remaining preserved lemon, minus its pulp,
into strips. Garnish the dish with the lemon and
the olives and serve at once.

tagines

chicken "mchermel"
serves 6 · preparation 10 minutes · cooking 25 minutes

3 onions
$^1/_4$ cup (60 mL) olive oil
1 whole chicken, weighing about 3 lb (1.5 kg), cut into pieces
$^1/_4$ tsp (1 mL) turmeric
pinch of saffron
$^1/_4$ tsp (1 mL) ground ginger
$1^3/_4$ cups (435 mL) water
4 cilantro stalks
4 parsley stalks
$^1/_4$ tsp (1 mL) ground cumin
$^1/_2$ tsp (2 mL) sweet paprika
2 cups (500 mL) green olives, pitted
1 lemon
2 preserved lemons
pinch of pepper
salt

Peel and finely chop the onions. Heat the olive oil in a large, heavy-based pot and brown the onions for 3 minutes. Add the chicken pieces to the pot and season with the turmeric, saffron, ginger, pepper, and salt to taste. Stir in $1^1/_4$ cups (310 mL) of the water, cover the pot, and let simmer over low heat for about 10 minutes.

Add the remaining water, the washed and snipped herbs, the cumin, and the paprika. Let reduce for about 10 minutes until the sauce has thickened. Add the well-rinsed olives, squeeze over the lemon juice, and let simmer for an additional 5 minutes.

Meanwhile, rinse the preserved lemons, cut them in half, and remove the pulp. Cut the rind into strips. Transfer the chicken to a serving platter, pour the sauce around it, and garnish with the strips of preserved lemon.

spicy stuffed chicken
serves 6 · preparation 30 minutes · cooking 65 minutes

3 garlic cloves
1 small red chili pepper
$1/4$ cup (60 mL) olive oil
1 lemon
1 Tbsp (15 mL) honey
3 Tbsp (45 mL) tomato juice
1 Tbsp (15 mL) cumin
1 Tbsp (15 mL) cracked niora peppercorns
1 Tbsp (15 mL) ground ginger
1 whole chicken, weighing about 3 lb (1.5 kg)
2 bay leaves
salt, pepper

FOR THE STUFFING
$1^{1}/_{2}$ cups (375 mL) raisins
1 garlic clove
1 onion
2 Tbsp (30 mL) butter
$1/2$ tsp (2 mL) cinnamon
$1/2$ tsp (2 mL) cumin
2 Tbsp (30 mL) skinned almonds
salt, pepper

Peel and chop the garlic and cut the chili into tiny rings. Make a sauce with the oil, garlic, chili, lemon juice, honey, tomato juice, and all the spices. Season to taste, mix well, and set aside.

To make the stuffing, soak the raisins in a little warm water.

Peel the garlic and onion and purée together in a blender. Melt the butter in a small pan and quickly brown the garlic and onion. Stir in the cinnamon and cumin and cook for about 2 minutes. Add the drained raisins and the almonds. Season to taste and cook for an additional 2 minutes. Set aside to cool.

Preheat the oven to 425°F (220°C/Gas 7).

Fill the cavity of the chicken with the stuffing. Place in an ovenproof pan and brush with the sauce. Place the bay leaves on top. Roast for about 1 hour, basting from time to time with the cooking juices.

Cut the chicken into pieces and serve hot with the stuffing and sauce.

tagines

roast chicken with chermola
serves 6 · preparation 20 minutes · marinating 60 minutes · cooking 45 minutes

3 garlic cloves
1 bunch of cilantro
1 lemon
1/2 tsp (2 mL) cumin
3/4 tsp (4 mL) paprika
pinch of cayenne pepper
3 Tbsp (45 mL) sunflower oil
1/2 tsp (2 mL) salt
3 small chicken (or young rooster), cut in two

Begin by making the marinade. Peel the garlic and wash the cilantro then chop together. Mix in a bowl with the lemon juice, spices, oil, and salt. Coat the chicken with half the marinade and refrigerate for 1 hour.

Preheat the oven to 425°F (220°C/Gas 7).

Transfer the chicken to an ovenproof pan, drizzle over the remaining marinade, and cook for about 45 minutes.

quail with raisins
serves 6 · preparation 10 minutes · cooking 30 minutes

3 large onions
2 Tbsp (30 mL) sunflower oil
1/4 cup (60 mL) butter
12 small quail
1 cinnamon stick
1/4 tsp (1 mL) ground ginger
pinch of saffron
2/3 cup (160 mL) water
2 cups (500 mL) raisins
1/2 tsp (2 mL) cinnamon
2 Tbsp (30 mL) sugar
2 Tbsp (30 mL) honey
1/4 tsp (1 mL) pepper
1/2 tsp (2 mL) salt

Peel and finely chop the onions. Heat the oil and half the butter in a large, heavy-based pot and soften the onions. Add the quail, cinnamon stick, ginger, saffron, and water and cook for 20 minutes.

Stir in the remaining butter, the raisins, cinnamon, sugar, honey, pepper, and salt. Let simmer until the sauce has reduced and has a good caramel color.

chicken with apricots
serves 6 · preparation 10 minutes · soaking 30 minutes · cooking 30 minutes

5 cups (1.25 L) dried apricots
1 onion
1/4 cup (60 mL) olive oil
pinch of saffron
1/2 tsp (2 mL) turmeric
1/2 tsp (2 mL) salt
1/4 tsp (1 mL) pepper
3 small chicken, cut in two, or 3 young rooster
1 1/4 cups (310 mL) water
2 Tbsp (30 mL) superfine sugar
handful of skinned almonds

Soak the apricots in a bowl of water for 30 minutes.

Peel and finely chop the onion. Heat the olive oil in a large, heavy-based pot and soften the onion for 2 minutes. Add the spices, salt, and pepper then place the chicken on top. Pour in the water and cook over low heat for 25 minutes.

When the chicken is cooked, take two ladlefuls of the cooking juices and put in a pan with the apricots and sugar. Cook for 3-4 minutes.

When the apricots have swelled, place the hot chicken on a serving platter and top with the sauce and apricots. Garnish with a few almonds.

dafina
serves 6 · preparation 20 minutes · cooking 24 hours

FOR THE MEATLOAF
1 onion
1/2 bunch of flat-leaf parsley
7 oz (200 g) ground beef
1 Tbsp (15 mL) cream of wheat
pinch of cinnamon
pinch of nutmeg
3 Tbsp (45 mL) all-purpose flour
2 eggs
salt, pepper
peanut oil

FOR THE WHEAT
1 head of garlic
1 cup (250 mL) wheat berries
1 Tbsp (15 mL) olive oil
salt, pepper

FOR THE RICE
1 cup (250 mL) rice
1 head of garlic
1 Tbsp (15 mL) olive oil
salt, pepper

14 oz (400 g) canned chickpeas
1 Tbsp (15 mL) sugar
1 1/4 cups (310 mL) olive oil
20 small potatoes
1 sweet potato
10 oz (300 g) stewing beef (chuck steak, round, etc)
14 oz (400 g) beef shank
1 calf's foot, cut into pieces
1 1/4 cups (310 mL) water
1 Tbsp (15 mL) baking soda
6 eggs
salt and pepper

Dafina is the dish traditionally eaten during the Shabbat, served midday Saturday. Cooking the dish begins on the Friday, before sunset, and it simmers away until the following day.

Early on the Friday afternoon, prepare the meatloaf. Peel the onion and finely mince with the parsley then mix with all the other ingredients except for the flour and 1 of the eggs. Form the mixture into an oval bread shape then roll it first in the flour, then in the beaten egg. Heat some oil in a skillet and fry the meat mixture on both sides. Remove and set aside.

Now prepare the wheat and rice. Remove the papery layer from the garlic head then combine all the ingredients for the wheat, put them in a piece of cheesecloth, and tie a knot in it to enclose. Do the same with the rice ingredients.

Put the chickpeas in a large stockpot or Dutch oven with the salt, pepper, and sugar. Cover with olive oil. Peel and wash the potatoes and the sweet potato and place on top. Pour in enough water to cover. Place the wheat and the rice in the pot, then the meats, the calf's foot, and the meatloaf. Season then pour over the measured water. Bring to a boil over medium heat then lower the heat to a simmer.

After 5 or 6 hours, sprinkle the baking soda into the pot. Wash the eggs and gently lower them into the pot, without breaking. Cover the pot and leave to cook all night. Just before you go to bed, check the water level and top up if necessary.

When you are ready to serve, remove and peel the eggs. Carefully lift out the meatloaf, the wheat, and the rice. Serve the wheat, the rice, and the chickpeas in separate bowls. Transfer the meats and the pieces of calf's foot to a serving platter; cut the meatloaf into slices and arrange on the platter too, along with the potatoes, the peeled eggs, and the sweet potato, cut into rounds.

TIP: If you cannot buy calf's foot, use an extra 7 oz (200 g) of beef shank.

tagines

meatballs in tomato sauce
serves 6 · preparation 15 minutes · cooking 15 minutes

1 onion
1 bunch of flat-leaf parsley
1 lb (500 g) ground beef or lamb (15% fat content)
1 Tbsp (15 mL) paprika
$1/2$ tsp (2 mL) cumin
3 Tbsp (45 mL) peanut oil
$1^1/4$ cups (310 mL) tomato juice
$1/4$ tsp (1 mL) tomato paste
1 cup (250 mL) water
6 eggs
salt, pepper

Peel and finely shred the onion. Wash and snip the parsley. Place in a large bowl with the meat, salt to taste, and half the paprika and cumin. Mix well and form into balls the size of a walnut. Set aside.

Pour the oil into a tagine and add the tomato juice, salt and pepper to taste, and the remaining spices. Cook for 2 minutes then add the tomato paste and water.

When the sauce bubbles, carefully place the meatballs in the tagine and stir until they are sealed on all sides. Break the eggs over the meatballs and leave to bubble gently over very low heat until the eggs are cooked.

Serve once the sauce has reduced.

tagines

lamb with fava beans
serves 6 • preparation 15 minutes • cooking 40 minutes

2¹/₂ lb (1.25 kg) leg or shoulder of lamb
1 onion
3 garlic cloves
3 Tbsp (45 mL) olive oil
³/₄ cup + 1 Tbsp (200 mL) water
¹/₂ tsp (2 mL) ground ginger
¹/₂ tsp (2 mL) turmeric
pinch of saffron
pinch of pepper
1 tied bunch of flat-leaf parsley
2 lb (1 kg) fresh or frozen fava beans
1 preserved lemon
1 cup (250 mL) green olives, pitted
salt

Cut the lamb into pieces and finely mince the onion and garlic. Heat the oil in a saucepan and cook the meat, onion, and garlic with salt to taste for 2 minutes. Add the water, the spices, and the parsley. Cover the pan and cook the meat for about 20 minutes.

Remove the lid, add the fava beans, and cook for 10 minutes. Cut the lemon into thin slices, add half to the pan, and cook for an additional 2 minutes.

Arrange the meat on a serving platter and garnish with the remaining lemon slices and the olives.

beef tenderloin maghdour
serves 6 • preparation 5 minutes • cooking 20 minutes

1 onion
2 lb (1 kg) beef tenderloin
¹/₂ cup (125 mL) butter
1 Tbsp (15 mL) paprika
¹/₂ tsp (2 mL) cumin
1¹/₄ cups (310 mL) water
1 bunch of flat-leaf parsley
1 Tbsp (15 mL) all-purpose flour
pinch of pepper
salt

Peel and finely slice the onion. Cut the meat into small cubes. Melt the butter in a large, heavy-based pot and brown the onion then add the meat, the spices, and salt to taste. Pour in the water and let simmer over low heat, stirring from time to time. Wash the parsley and snip over the meat.

Meanwhile, blend the flour with about ²/₃ cup (160 mL) water. When the meat is cooked, stir this into the pot and stir gently to prevent lumps forming.

Tip: You can use rib or short loin instead of tenderloin.

veal shank in tomato sauce
serves 6 • preparation 15 minutes • cooking 50 minutes

2 lb (1 kg) veal shank
1 large onion
2 garlic cloves
3 Tbsp (45 mL) olive oil
¹/₂ tsp (2 mL) pepper
1 Tbsp (15 mL) turmeric
pinch of saffron
1³/₄ cups + 1 Tbsp (450 mL) water
3 lb (1.5 kg) tomatoes
1 Tbsp (15 mL) paprika
1 bunch of flat-leaf parsley
salt

Cut the meat into pieces and finely mince the onion and garlic. Heat the oil in a large, heavy-based pot and add the onion, garlic, salt to taste, pepper, turmeric, and saffron. Pour in two-thirds of the water and, when the liquid boils, add the meat to the pot. Let it cook for 5 minutes then pour in the remaining water, cover with the lid, and let simmer over low heat for 40 minutes.

Meanwhile, blanch the tomatoes by dropping them in a bowl of boiling water for 4 minutes then skin them, squeeze out the juice, and cut the flesh into quarters.

When the meat is almost cooked, add the tomatoes, paprika, and the washed and snipped parsley. Let simmer for an additional 10 minutes.

tagines

lamb with quince
serves 6 · preparation 20 minutes · cooking 30 minutes

2¹/₂ lb (1.25 kg) leg or shoulder of lamb
2 onions
1 cup (250 mL) water
2 Tbsp (30 mL) peanut oil
¹/₄ cup (60 mL) butter
1 cinnamon stick
pinch of saffron
¹/₂ tsp (2 mL) ground ginger
2 lb (1 kg) quince
¹/₂ tsp (2 mL) cinnamon
2 Tbsp (30 mL) sugar
2 Tbsp (30 mL) honey
pinch of pepper
salt

Cut the lamb into pieces and peel and finely chop the onions. Put in a large, heavy-based pot with the water, oil, half the butter, the cinnamon stick, saffron, and ginger. Season, then cover the pot and cook over medium heat for 20 minutes.

Meanwhile peel and core the quince and cut into eighths. Put the remaining butter, the cinnamon, sugar, and honey in a saucepan and moisten with 2 ladlefuls of the cooking juices from the pot. Tip in the quince and cook until they are caramelized.

Transfer the meat to a round plate and serve with the sauce and the quince.

lamb with peas and sunchokes
serves 6 · preparation 10 minutes · cooking 40 minutes

2¹/₂ lb (1.25 kg) leg or shoulder of lamb
1 large onion
2 garlic cloves
3 Tbsp (45 mL) olive oil
¹/₂ tsp (2 mL) turmeric
pinch of saffron
¹/₂ tsp (2 mL) ground ginger
1³/₄ cups + 1 Tbsp (450 mL) water
2 lb (1 kg) fresh or frozen peas
10 fresh or frozen sunchoke hearts
1 preserved lemon
1 cup (250 mL) green olives, pitted
salt, pepper

Cut the meat into pieces and peel and finely chop the onion and garlic. Pour the oil into a large, heavy-based pot and tip in the onion, garlic, spices, and salt and pepper to taste. Add two-thirds of the water and stir until the mixture is evenly blended.

Put the pot on the heat, add the meat, cover, and let cook over medium heat for about 15 minutes.

After this time, add the remaining water, let it come to a simmer, then add the peas and sunchokes. Cook for about 10 minutes over low heat. When the sauce has reduced and the vegetables are cooked, remove from the heat.

Serve on a round serving plate, garnished with strips of preserved lemon and the olives.

lamb with apricots
serves 6 · preparation 20 minutes · cooking 1 hour 15 minutes

2¹/₂ lb (1.25 kg) shoulder of lamb
1 orange
1 cup (250 mL) dried apricots
1 large onion
2 Tbsp (30 mL) olive oil
¹/₂ tsp (2 mL) cumin
¹/₄ tsp (1 mL) cinnamon
1 Tbsp (15 mL) powdered almonds
1¹/₄ cups (310 mL) water
1 Tbsp (15 mL) white sesame seeds
¹/₂ bunch of cilantro (optional)
salt, pepper

Cut the meat into pieces. Wash the orange then zest the rind. Squeeze the juice and soak the apricots in the juice to swell. Peel and finely slice the onion.

Heat the oil in a large, heavy-based pot and brown the onion for about 10 minutes, stirring from time to time.

Add the meat, cumin, cinnamon, and salt and pepper to taste and stir well for 5 minutes. Pour in the orange juice with the apricots, orange juice, almonds, and water. Cover, and simmer over medium heat. When the juice is bubbling, lower the heat and continue to cook, stirring from time to time.

Meanwhile, dry-toast the sesame seeds in a skillet. They should become golden but not blackened.

When the lamb is cooked, after about 40 minutes, transfer to a serving platter and sprinkle with the sesame seeds and snipped cilantro, if using.

tagines

lamb with white truffles
serves 6 • preparation 15 minutes • cooking 25 minutes

2¹/₂ lb (1.25 kg) leg or shoulder of lamb
1 onion
2 garlic cloves
¹/₄ cup (60 mL) olive oil
1¹/₂ cups (375 mL) water
¹/₂ tsp (2 mL) ground ginger
pinch of saffron
1 small can white truffles, drained
   (or ¹/₂ lb/250 g mushrooms, trimmed and quartered)
¹/₂ bunch of flat-leaf parsley
¹/₂ bunch of cilantro
salt, pepper

Cut the meat into pieces and peel and finely mince the onion and garlic. Heat the olive oil in a large, heavy-based pot and cook the meat, onion, and garlic together for 2 minutes. Add the water, ginger, saffron, and salt and pepper to taste. Cover and cook for 15 minutes.

Add the drained truffles (or mushrooms), and the washed and snipped parsley and cilantro. Let simmer for an additional 5-7 minutes over low heat until the sauce has reduced.

Transfer to a serving platter, with the meat arranged around the truffles.

"mderbel" tagine with eggplant
serves 6 • preparation 15 minutes • cooking 40 minutes

2 medium eggplants
2¹/₂ lb (1.25 kg) shoulder of lamb
1 large onion
4 garlic cloves
oil for frying
¹/₂ tsp (2 mL) paprika
¹/₂ tsp (2 mL) cumin
¹/₂ lemon
3 Tbsp (45 mL) olive oil
¹/₂ tsp (2 mL) turmeric
pinch of saffron
¹/₂ tsp (2 mL) ground ginger
¹/₄ tsp (1 mL) pepper
1¹/₄ cups (310 mL) water
salt

Wash and trim the eggplants and cut into thick slices. Cut the meat into pieces, and peel and finely mince the onion and 3 of the garlic cloves.

Heat the oil and fry the eggplants on both sides then remove and drain. Cut them roughly into smaller pieces then brown off in a skillet with the paprika, cumin, the remaining garlic clove, peeled and crushed, and a little salt. Remove from the heat and squeeze in the lemon juice.

Heat the olive oil in a heavy-based pot and brown the minced onion and garlic, and the remaining spices. Add the meat then pour in the water. Cover and let simmer for about 30 minutes. Remove the lid and reduce the sauce until thick.

Arrange the meat on a plate and serve the eggplant mixture on top.

tagines

bundegas with olives
serves 6 • preparation 15 minutes • cooking 20 minutes

2 cups (500 mL) purple olives
piece of dry bread
1 bunch of flat-leaf parsley
1 bunch of cilantro
2 onions
2 garlic cloves
1 preserved lemon
1^1/$_2$ lb (800 g) ground beef
^{1}/$_2$ tsp (2 mL) cumin
1 Tbsp (15 mL) cracked niora peppercorns
1 egg
^{1}/$_4$ cup (60 mL) olive oil
^{3}/$_4$ cup + 1 Tbsp (200 mL) water
^{1}/$_2$ tsp (2 mL) turmeric
pinch of saffron
salt, pepper

Boil the olives in a pan of water for 5 minutes then drain and pit them.

Meanwhile, soak the bread in warm water. Wash the herbs, peel and chop the onions, peel and slice the garlic, and remove the pulp from the lemon then cut the rind into thin strips.

Mince together the squeezed-out bread, the parsley, onions, meat, salt and pepper to taste, cumin, niora, and the egg. Form into small balls the size of a walnut and set aside.

Heat the oil in a large, heavy-based pot with the water, turmeric, saffron, garlic, and preserved lemon. Bring to a boil then carefully lower the meatballs into the liquid and simmer, covered, for 15 minutes. Add the pitted olives and snipped cilantro and reduce the sauce for 5 minutes.

rabbit with spicy sauce
serves 6 • preparation 15 minutes • cooking 25 minutes

1 prepared rabbit, cut into 8
1 large onion
3 garlic cloves
3 Tbsp (45 mL) olive oil
1 Tbsp (15 mL) paprika
^{1}/$_2$ tsp (2 mL) cumin
pinch of cayenne pepper
^{1}/$_4$ tsp (1 mL) pepper
1^1/$_4$ cups (310 mL) water
2 Tbsp (30 mL) vinegar
coarse salt

Rub the rabbit pieces with the salt. Soak in water for several minutes.

Peel and chop the onion and crush the garlic. Heat the oil in a pot and soften the onion and garlic for 2 minutes. Add the drained rabbit and the spices. Pour in the water and simmer over low heat for 20 minutes. When the sauce has reduced, remove from the heat and stir in the vinegar.

veal with chickpeas and onions
serves 6 • preparation 15 minutes • cooking 55 minutes

2 lb (1 kg) veal shank
3 large onions
3 Tbsp (45 mL) olive oil
^{1}/$_4$ cup (60 mL) butter
^{1}/$_2$ tsp (2 mL) ground ginger
^{1}/$_2$ tsp (2 mL) turmeric
pinch of saffron
^{1}/$_4$ tsp (1 mL) pepper
2 cups (500 mL) water
2 cups (500 mL) canned, drained chickpeas
1 bunch of flat-leaf parsley
salt

Cut the meat into pieces and peel and finely slice the onions. Heat the oil and butter in a large, heavy-based pot and add the onions. Soften for 2 minutes then add the meat and the spices. Pour in ^{1}/$_2$ cup (125 mL) of the water and cook for 5 minutes, stirring with a spatula.

Stir the chickpeas in with the remaining water and the snipped parsley. Cover and let simmer for about 30 minutes, then remove the lid and let bubble for 5 minutes. The sauce should be fairly thin but not liquid.

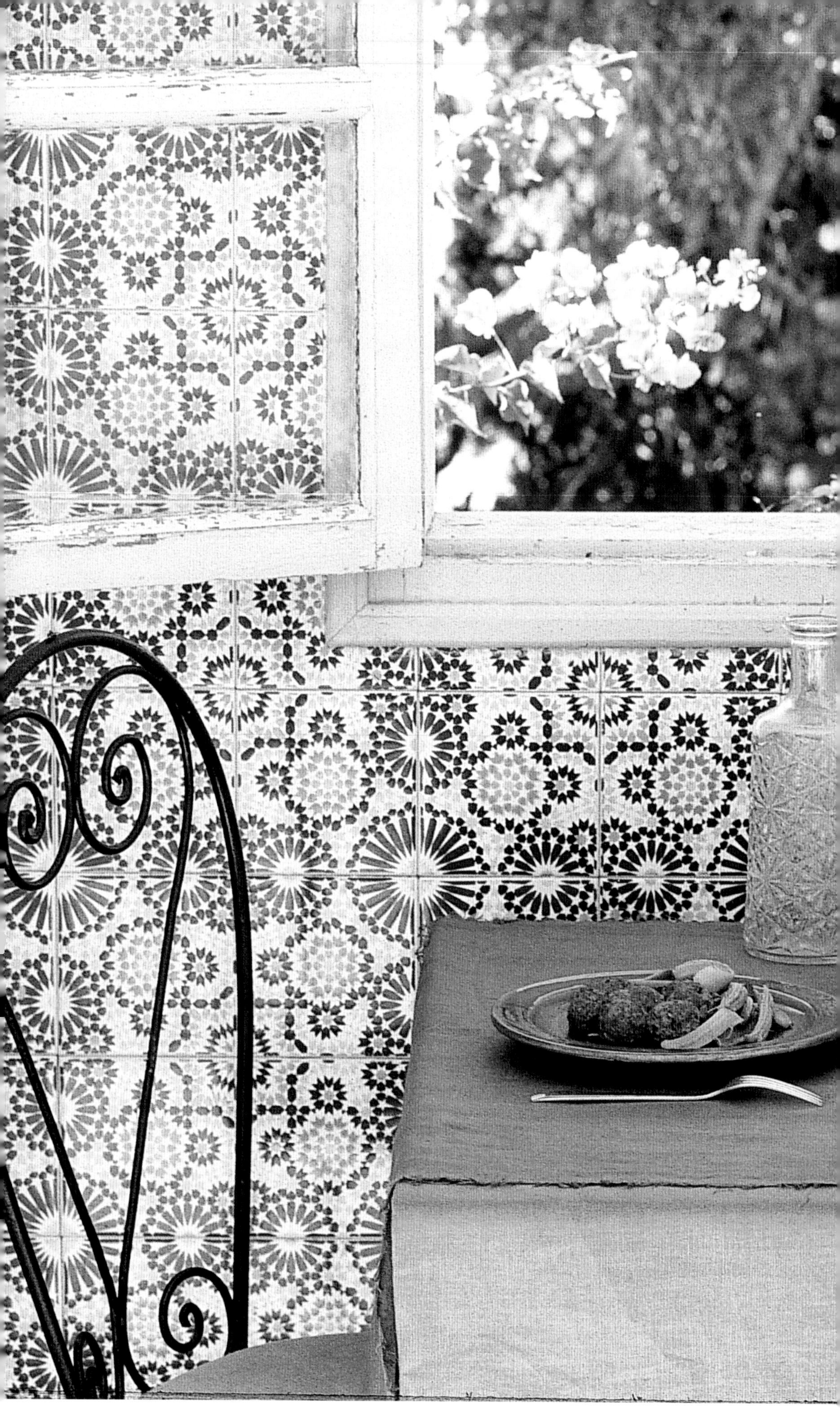

beef meatballs with cardoons
serves 6 · preparation 35 minutes · cooking 30 minutes

2 heads of fresh cardoons
1 lemon
2 onions
4 garlic cloves
1 bunch of flat-leaf parsley
1 piece of dry bread
2 lb (1 kg) ground beef
1 egg
$^1/_2$ Tbsp cracked niora peppercorns
$^1/_2$ tsp (2 mL) cumin
$^1/_2$ tsp (2 mL) ground ginger
5 Tbsp olive oil
$^3/_4$ cup + 1 Tbsp (200 mL) water
$^1/_2$ tsp (2 mL) turmeric
pinch of saffron
salt, pepper

String the cardoons and place in a bowl of water with the lemon juice added to it. Peel the onions and garlic, wash the parsley, and soak the bread in warm water.

Mince together the onions, 2 of the garlic cloves, the parsley, and the squeezed-out bread to form a paste. Mix this with the meat in a bowl. Add the egg, niora, cumin, ginger, and salt and pepper to taste. Mix thoroughly and form into balls about the size of a walnut.

Heat the oil in a large, heavy-based pot with the water, turmeric, saffron, and the remaining 2 garlic cloves, finely sliced. Bring to a boil then carefully lower the meatballs into the liquid and simmer, covered, over low heat for 20 minutes.

Drain the cardoons, cut into short lengths, and put into the pot 15 minutes before the end of cooking time.

fish

return to fish

The fish most used in Moroccan cuisine are gilt-head bream, mullet, tuna, whiting, sea bass, cod, pollock, and hake, but also swordfish and pandora or red sea bream, and not forgetting the indispensable sardine, the bounty of the Moroccan seas, which can never be bettered than simply served grilled.

All these fish can be baked in the oven, fried, stuffed, turned into fishballs, or simmered in a tagine with vegetables.

spliced sardines/sardines "in wedlock"
serves 6 · preparation 15 minutes · marinating 1 hour · cooking 15 minutes

36 sardines
4 garlic cloves
$1/2$ bunch of flat-leaf parsley
1 large bunch of cilantro
1 lemon
1 Tbsp (15 mL) paprika
1 Tbsp (15 mL) cumin
pinch of cayenne pepper
$3/4$ cup (185 mL) all-purpose flour
$1/2$ tsp (2 mL) salt
oil for frying

Ask your supplier to fillet and butterfly the sardines for you.

Rinse the sardines and let them drain while you prepare the marinade. Chop the garlic, parsley, and cilantro, tip into a large bowl, and add the lemon juice, salt, and the spices.

Coat the fillets with marinade on both sides, then press them together in pairs, underside to underside. Lay on a plate, drizzle over the remaining marinade, cover with plastic wrap, and marinate in the refrigerator for 1 hour.

Heat the oil in a large skillet, dredge the sardines with flour on both sides, and fry over low heat, turning once. Transfer to paper towels to absorb the excess oil before arranging on a serving platter.

fish

stuffed squid
serves 6 · preparation 15 minutes · cooking 20 minutes

6 medium squid (about 5 inches/12 cm long)
1 bunch of flat-leaf parsley
1 bunch of cilantro
5 oz (150 g) ground beef
2/3 cup (160 mL) cooked rice
1/4 tsp (1 mL) pepper
1 Tbsp (15 mL) paprika
1/2 cup (125 mL) tomato juice
2 Tbsp (30 mL) olive oil
2 garlic cloves, peeled and sliced
1/4 tsp (1 mL) cumin
2/3 cup (160 mL) water
1/2 tsp (2 mL) tomato paste
salt
toothpicks

Wash and clean the squid and set aside. Wash and snip the parsley and cilantro separately.

In a large bowl mix together the meat, parsley, rice, salt to taste, pepper, and half the paprika. Stuff the squid pouches and secure with a toothpick.

Put the tomato juice into a large, heavy-based pot with the oil, garlic, cilantro, cumin, and the remaining paprika. Pour in the water and bring to a simmer. Add the squid and the tomato paste, cover, and simmer for 20 minutes.

The squid should be tender and the sauce reduced.

shrimp "pil-pil"
serves 6 · preparation 5 minutes · cooking 10 minutes

1 lb (500 g) raw jumbo shrimp
2 garlic cloves
1/4 cup (60 mL) peanut oil
1 Tbsp (15 mL) snipped flat-leaf parsley
1/2 tsp (2 mL) paprika
1/2 level tsp salt
2 fresh red chili peppers to garnish

Shell the shrimp and peel and roughly chop the garlic.

Heat the oil in a skillet or tagine over medium heat. Add the shrimp, garlic, parsley, paprika, and salt. Stir gently, turning to cook on both sides, then add the chili peppers to garnish the dish. Serve hot.

fishball tagine
serves 6 · preparation 20 minutes · cooking 20 minutes

FOR THE FISHBALLS
2 lb (1 kg) any white fish
2 garlic cloves
1 bunch of cilantro
2 eggs, beaten
1 Tbsp (15 mL) sweet paprika
3 Tbsp (45 mL) olive oil
salt, pepper

FOR THE SAUCE
2 cups (500 mL) tomato juice
1 garlic clove
1/2 tsp (2 mL) sweet paprika
3 Tbsp (45 mL) olive oil
2/3 cup (160 mL) water
salt, pepper

Prepare the sauce by mixing together all the ingredients except the water in a large pot. Stir in the water and cook over low heat for 10 minutes.

Meanwhile, prepare the fishballs. Mince the fish with the garlic and the washed cilantro. Mix together in a bowl with the beaten eggs, paprika, seasoning, and olive oil. Form into balls the size of walnuts.

Carefully lower the fishballs into the bubbling sauce. Add a little extra water and cook over low heat for 10 minutes.

hake with saffron
serves 6 • preparation 10 minutes • cooking 15 minutes

1 bunch of cilantro
4 garlic cloves
1/2 tsp (2 mL) ground ginger
1/2 tsp (2 mL) turmeric
2 pinches of saffron
6 hake steaks
3 Tbsp (45 mL) olive oil
1/2 cup (125 mL) water
1 tomato
1 preserved lemon
salt

Wash the cilantro, peel the garlic, and finely mince together. Put in a bowl with the spices. Wash the fish, coat with the spice mixture, and set aside.

Pour the oil and water into a large pot. Place over the heat and bring to a gentle boil before carefully lowering in the fish. Cook over low heat for about 15 minutes. Skin the tomato and cut into tiny pieces and slice the preserved lemon into strips. Add to the pot.

When the sauce is thick, remove the pot from the heat and carefully lift out the fish.

stuffed pandora (red sea bream)
serves 6 • preparation 15 minutes • cooking 65 minutes

1 whole pandora weighing about 3 lb (1.5 kg),
    cleaned and scaled
14 oz (400 g) hake fillet
1 bunch of flat-leaf parsley
2 celery stalks
1 red bell pepper
1 preserved lemon
3 garlic cloves
2 Tbsp (30 mL) sunflower oil
2 cups (500 mL) cooked rice
1/2 tsp (2 mL) turmeric
pinch of saffron
1/2 tsp (2 mL) ground ginger
1 lemon
2 Tbsp (30 mL) olive oil
3/4 cup + 1 Tbsp (200 mL) water
pinch of pepper
salt

Mince together the hake, parsley, celery, bell pepper, preserved lemon, and garlic. Heat 1 Tbsp (15 mL) of the sunflower oil in a skillet, add the mixture, and cook over low heat, stirring, for 3 minutes. Remove from the pan and let cool.

Put the rice, spices, and half the lemon juice in a bowl then add the cooled hake mixture and combine.

Preheat the oven to 350°F (180°C/Gas 4).

Rub the pandora with the remaining lemon juice, season with salt and pepper, and drizzle over 1 Tbsp (15 mL) olive oil then fill with the stuffing.

Put the remaining sunflower and olive oil in a shallow ovenproof casserole dish, pour in the water, and place the stuffed fish in the casserole. Transfer to the oven and cook for 1 hour.

sea bream with olives
serves 6 • preparation 20 minutes • cooking 60 minutes

1 whole sea bream, weighing about 4 lb (2 kg),
    cleaned and scaled
3 tomatoes
3 celery stalks
1 bunch of flat-leaf parsley
2 preserved lemons
3 garlic cloves
5 potatoes
1/2 tsp (2 mL) turmeric
1/2 tsp (2 mL) pepper
2 cups (500 mL) cooked rice
2 cups (500 mL) green olives, pitted
3 Tbsp (45 mL) olive oil
salt

Wash the fish thoroughly then slash twice on both sides. Skin the tomatoes and cut them into small pieces. Wash the celery and the parsley and finely chop. Quarter the preserved lemons, remove the pulp, and finely slice the rind. Peel and mince the garlic. Peel and slice the potatoes.

Prepare a marinade with the tomatoes, celery, parsley, lemon rind, garlic, turmeric, pepper, salt to taste, and a large glass of water. Add half the mixture to the cooked rice with half the olives. Fill the fish with this stuffing.

Preheat the oven to 350°F (180°C/Gas 4).

Put the oil and the remaining marinade into a baking pan and place the fish in the middle with the sliced potatoes around it. Stir well to coat the potatoes in the sauce. Transfer to the oven and cook for 1 hour. Serve garnished with the remaining olives.

tangiers-style anchovies
serves 6 · preparation 35 minutes · cooking 10 minutes

2 lb (1 kg) fresh anchovies
6 garlic cloves
1 bunch of flat-leaf parsley
1 bunch of cilantro
2 Tbsp (30 mL) paprika
2 Tbsp (30 mL) cumin
1/4 cup (60 mL) vinegar
2 Tbsp (30 mL) water
1/4 cup (60 mL) olive oil
2 Tbsp (30 mL) ground thyme leaves

Wash the anchovies and remove the spine to leave two fillets, but without separating them. Lay them flat in a bowl.

Preheat the oven to 350°F (180°C/Gas 4).

Peel and chop the garlic. Wash the herbs and chop finely. Prepare a marinade with all the ingredients except the olive oil and thyme. Dip each prepared anchovy on both sides first in the marinade, then in the olive oil, close the two fillets together, and arrange them in a single layer in a baking pan or tagine.

Pour the remaining marinade over the anchovies and sprinkle with the thyme. Transfer the pan to the oven for 10 minutes or place the tagine over a very low heat.

To serve this dish as an appetizer, halve the quantities.

kabobs and accompaniments

kabobs and accompaniments

beef kabobs
serves 6 · preparation 15 minutes · resting 1 hour · cooking 5 minutes

2¹/₄ lb (1.2 kg) beef tenderloin
1 large onion
1 bunch of flat-leaf parsley
¹/₄ tsp (1 mL) pepper
salt
skewers

Cube the beef. Peel and roughly chop the onion, and wash and snip the parsley. Mix everything together in a bowl, season, then cover with plastic wrap and place in the refrigerator for 1 hour.

Thread the beef onto the skewers and cook for 5 minutes, turning regularly, over hot coals or on a grill or broiler.

kabobs and accompaniments

calf's liver kabobs
serves 6 • preparation 15 minutes • resting 1 hour • cooking 8 minutes

2 lb (1 kg) calf's liver, cut in thick slices
5 oz (150 g) beef caul fat
1 tsp (5 mL) cumin
1 Tbsp (15 mL) paprika
1/4 tsp (1 mL) pepper
salt
skewers

Quickly broil the liver slices on both sides. Cut the liver and fat into pieces and put in a bowl with the spices and salt. Cover with plastic wrap and place in the refrigerator for 1 hour.

Thread the liver onto the skewers, alternating with two pieces of fat on each skewer, and cook for 5 minutes, turning regularly, over hot coals or on a grill or broiler.

meatball kabobs
serves 6 • preparation 25 minutes • cooking 3 minutes

1 large onion
1 bunch of flat-leaf parsley
1 bunch of cilantro
1 mint stalk
2 lb (1 kg) ground beef
1 Tbsp (15 mL) paprika
1 tsp (5 mL) cumin
pinch of ras-el-hanout
salt
skewers

Peel the onion, wash the herbs, and mince finely together. Transfer to a bowl with the beef, spices, and salt to taste and mix thoroughly. Form into 24 balls each about 1½ inches (4 cm) across, then flatten slightly and thread four on each skewer. (You can also flatten them completely to form small burgers.)

Cook for 5 minutes, turning regularly, over hot coals or on a grill or broiler.

lamb kabobs
serves 6 • preparation 15 minutes • resting 2 hours • cooking 5 minutes

2 lb (1 kg) boneless leg of lamb
1 onion
1 bunch of flat-leaf parsley
1 tsp (5 mL) cumin
1 Tbsp (15 mL) paprika
1/4 tsp (1 mL) pepper
salt
skewers

Cube the meat. Peel and roughly chop the onion, and wash and snip the parsley. Mix everything together in a bowl, season, then cover with plastic wrap and place in the refrigerator for 2 hours.

Thread the lamb onto the skewers and cook for 5 minutes, turning regularly, over hot coals or on a grill or broiler.

tripe in sauce
serves 6 · preparation 15 minutes · cooking 30 minutes

1 lb (500 g) cooked tripe
8 oz (250 g) calf's liver
2 garlic cloves
3 Tbsp (45 mL) olive oil
1 Tbsp (15 mL) paprika
pinch of cayenne pepper
1¼ cups (310 mL) water
2 Tbsp (30 mL) vinegar
salt

Cut the tripe and liver into pieces. Peel and crush the garlic. Heat the oil in a heavy-based pot, add the garlic and the spices, and stir well. Pour in the water then add the tripe and liver. Season, cover the pot, and cook over medium heat for 20 minutes.

Remove the lid and add the vinegar. If the sauce seems too liquid, let reduce over low heat. Serve very hot.

kidneys with rice
serves 6 · preparation 10 minutes · cooking 30 minutes

1 lb (500 g) beef kidneys
2 small onions
1 tied bunch of flat-leaf parsley
¼ cup (60 mL) butter
1 Tbsp (15 mL) peanut oil
1¼ cups (310 mL) water
½ tsp (2 mL) ground ginger
½ tsp (2 mL) turmeric
pinch of saffron
¼ tsp (1 mL) pepper
1½ cups (375 mL) rice
salt

Trim the kidneys and cut into pieces. Peel and chop the onions. Wash the parsley. Heat the butter and oil in a heavy-based pot and brown the onion. Add the water and bring to a boil, then add the spices, salt to taste, kidneys, and parsley.

Cook over medium heat for 20 minutes then tip in the rice and enough water to cover. Cook for 10 minutes until the rice has absorbed all the water.

Arrange on a large serving platter.

calf's kidney kabobs
serves 6 · preparation 15 minutes · resting 1 hour · cooking 5 minutes

2 lb (1 kg) calf's kidneys
½ tsp (2 mL) cumin
1 Tbsp (15 mL) paprika
¼ tsp (1 mL) pepper
salt
skewers

Trim the kidneys and cut into cubes. Put in a bowl with the spices and salt to taste, stir by hand to coat, then cover with plastic wrap and place in the refrigerator for 1 hour.

Thread the kidneys onto the skewers and cook for 5 minutes, turning regularly, over hot coals or on a grill or broiler.

VARIATION: You can also make heart kabobs following this recipe.

kabobs and accompaniments

potatoes "mchermel"
serves 6 • preparation 15 minutes • cooking 20 minutes

2 lb (1 kg) potatoes
1 bunch of flat-leaf parsley
1 bunch of cilantro
3 garlic cloves
3 Tbsp (45 mL) olive oil
1 Tbsp (15 mL) paprika
1/2 tsp (2 mL) cumin
pinch of cayenne pepper
1 1/4 cups (310 mL) water
salt

Peel and wash the potatoes, then cut into medium-sized pieces. Wash the herbs, peel the garlic, and chop together.

Heat the oil in a heavy-based pot. Add the chopped herbs and garlic, cook for 2 minutes, then add the potatoes.

Cook for 3 minutes, add the spices and salt to taste, then pour in the water. Cover the pot, lower the heat, then let cook for 15 minutes. The sauce should be reduced.

green lentils with tomato sauce
serves 6 • preparation 15 minutes • cooking 25 minutes

1 onion
2 garlic cloves
3 tomatoes
3 Tbsp (45 mL) olive oil
3/4 cup + 1 Tbsp (200 mL) water
1/2 tsp (2 mL) tomato paste
1 lb (500 g) green lentils
1/2 tsp (2 mL) paprika
1 red bell pepper
1 bunch of flat-leaf parsley
salt, pepper

Peel the onion and garlic and finely mince together. Skin and crush the tomatoes. Heat the oil in a heavy-based pot and cook the onion, garlic, and tomatoes for 10 minutes. Add the water, stir in the tomato paste, then add the lentils, paprika, and salt and pepper to taste.

Wash the bell pepper, core, trim, and roughly chop. Wash and snip the parsley. Add both to the pot and continue to cook over low heat for 10 minutes. Let the sauce reduce.

vegetable tagine
serves 6 • preparation 10 minutes • cooking 20 minutes

2 zucchini
2 carrots
5 oz (150 g) cauliflower
5 oz (150 g) broccoli
6 sunchoke hearts
2 preserved lemons
1 bunch of cilantro
1/4 cup (60 mL) olive oil
1 cup (250 mL) chopped onion
1 cup (250 mL) shelled fava beans
1 cup (250 mL) shelled peas
1 cup (250 mL) chopped green beans
2/3 cup (160 mL) water
1 cup (250 mL) lemon-marinated olives
1/2 tsp (2 mL) turmeric
1/4 tsp (1 mL) pepper
1/4 tsp (1 mL) salt

Wash the zucchini, carrots, cauliflower, and broccoli. Trim and cut the zucchini and carrots into short sticks and chop the cauliflower and broccoli into florets. Cut the sunchokes into quarters or sixths, depending on size. Cut the preserved lemons into fine strips and wash and snip the cilantro.

Heat the oil in a large, heavy-based pot and soften the onions for 5 minutes. Add, in this order, the carrots, the fava beans, the cauliflower, the broccoli, and the sunchokes, then the peas, the green beans, and the zucchini. Season with salt and pepper and pour in the water.

After 10 minutes, add the preserved lemon strips, cilantro, olives, and turmeric. Let cook over low heat for 5 minutes before serving.

zucchini with tomatoes
serves 6 • preparation 10 minutes • cooking 20 minutes

2 lb (1 kg) zucchini
1 onion
3 tomatoes
3 Tbsp (45 mL) olive oil
3 garlic cloves
1 Tbsp (15 mL) paprika
1 cup (250 mL) water
salt

Wash the zucchini and cut into rounds. Peel and finely slice the onion and cut the tomatoes into cubes. Heat the oil in a heavy-based pot, add the onion and tomato, and soften for 5 minutes. Add the garlic, paprika, and salt to taste and pour in the water.

When the sauce is simmering, add the zucchini and cook for 15 minutes.

Remove from the heat once the sauce has reduced.

coyscoys

couscous and pulses

It is tempting to use precooked couscous in a couscous dish—it's true that there are good-quality versions around and that they will save you time—but the traditional method is also part of the pleasure of Moroccan cuisine, and mastering it is not as complicated as it seems. If you can, use medium-grain, dry couscous (sold in bulk). As for chickpeas, don't hesitate to forgo the soaking stage and buy without guilt a quality brand, prepared and canned!

how to make couscous

3 cups (750 mL) medium-grain couscous • 1 Tbsp (15 mL) salt • 1 Tbsp (15 mL) sunflower oil • 2 cups (500 mL) cold water • 3 Tbsp (45 mL) softened butter

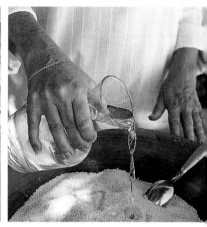

ip the couscous into a wide, shallow
wl or tray so that it can be spread out.

2 Add the salt and pour over the oil,
stirring it in with a fork to keep the
grains separate.

3 Gradually sprinkle with the water.
Let the couscous grains swell for
5 minutes, then coat your hands with
sunflower oil and work through the
couscous, lifting and aerating it.

et the couscous rest for 10 minutes,
asionally aerating it with your
ers so that it doesn't stick.

5 Tip the couscous into the upper
section of a couscous steamer and
place above boiling bouillon. Check
that the two sections of the steamer
are tightly fitted together to ensure
the steam doesn't escape.

6 Make little holes in the couscous
with the tip of a wooden spoon.

s soon as the steam starts to
ape, transfer the couscous to the
de, shallow bowl. Sprinkle with a
ss of water and aerate again, this
e with a wooden spoon to avoid
rning yourself.

8 Return the couscous to the upper
section of the couscous steamer
and repeat the cooking instructions
in steps 6-7, then add the softened
butter. Aerate the couscous with your
hands again, incorporating the butter.

9 Again let it rest for a few moments
then separate the grains, mixing the
couscous with both hands to distribute
the butter thoroughly.

couscous with seven vegetables
serves 6 · preparation 20 minutes · cooking 40 minutes

3 lb (1.5 kg) boneless shoulder of lamb
3 onions
1/3 cup (80 mL) butter, half for the meat, half for the couscous
1/4 cup (60 mL) olive oil
1/2 tsp (2 mL) ground ginger
1/2 tsp (2 mL) turmeric
pinch of saffron
1/2 tsp (2 mL) pepper
7 cups (1.75 L) water
8 oz (250 g) carrots
8 oz (250 g) turnips
1 small green cabbage
1 green bell pepper
8 oz (250 g) shelled fava beans
2 tomatoes
4 potatoes
8 oz (250 g) small zucchini
1 tied bunch of cilantro
3 cups (750 mL) medium-grain couscous
1 Tbsp (15 mL) salt

Cut the meat into cubes. Peel and finely chop the onions. Heat half the butter and the oil in the base of a couscous steamer and add the meat, onion, and all the spices.

When the meat is browned on all sides, add 2 cups (500 mL) of the water. When it boils, add another 4 cups (1 L) of the water and the salt. Cover the pan.

Let cook for 20 minutes then add the remaining water. Peel and quarter the carrots and turnips and add to the pot. Trim, core, and quarter the cabbage and bell pepper and add, along with the fava beans. Check the seasoning and continue to cook for 10 minutes.

Halve the tomatoes, peel and halve the potatoes, and quarter the zucchini. Add everything to the pot with the bunch of cilantro and let simmer for 10 minutes.

Meanwhile, prepare the couscous following the steps on page 109, placing the couscous over the base of the couscous steamer when you add the vegetables to the meat.

Serve as soon as the couscous is ready.

couscous with raisins and chickpeas
serves 6 · preparation 15 minutes · cooking 30 minutes

3 lb (1.5 kg) boneless shoulder of lamb
4 onions
1/3 cup (80 mL) butter, half for the meat,
    half for the couscous
1/4 cup (60 mL) olive oil
1 1/2 cups (375 mL) canned, drained chickpeas
1/2 tsp (2 mL) ground ginger
1/2 tsp (2 mL) turmeric
pinch of saffron
1/2 tsp (2 mL) pepper
1/2 tsp (2 mL) salt
4 cups (1 L) water
3 cups (750 mL) raisins
3 cups (750 mL) medium-grain couscous

Cut the meat into cubes. Peel and finely chop
the onions. Heat half the butter and the oil in a
couscous steamer. Add the meat and onion.

When the meat is browned on all sides, add the
chickpeas and the spices and salt. Pour in the
water, cover, and let cook for 20 minutes. Add the
raisins and cook for an additional 5 minutes.

Meanwhile, prepare the couscous following the
method on page 109.

Transfer the couscous to a large shallow serving
dish, arrange the meat in the center, and top with
the bouillon, the raisins, and the chickpeas.

winter couscous with zucchini
Serves 6 · preparation 20 minutes · cooking 35 minutes

3 lb (1.5 kg) boneless veal shank
2 onions
1/2 cup (125 mL) butter, half for the meat, half for
    the couscous
2 Tbsp (30 mL) olive oil
1/2 tsp (2 mL) ground ginger
1/2 tsp (2 mL) turmeric
pinch of saffron
1/2 tsp (2 mL) pepper
1 Tbsp (15 mL) salt
1 lb (500 g) zucchini
10 oz (300 g) turnips
8 oz (250 g) pumpkin
2 1/2 cups (625 mL) shelled fava beans
1 bunch of cilantro
3 cups (750 mL) medium-grain couscous
2 cups (500 mL) milk

Cut the meat into cubes. Peel and finely chop the
onions. Heat half the butter and the oil in a heavy-
based pot and soften the onions. Add the meat
and brown on all sides. Add the spices, salt, and
enough water to cover. Put the lid on the pot and
cook for 20 minutes. Meanwhile, peel and chop the
vegetables and wash the cilantro. Add to the pot
and cook for an additional 15 minutes.

Meanwhile, prepare the couscous following the
method on page 109.

Transfer the couscous to a large shallow serving dish
and arrange the meat and vegetables in the center.
Pour the milk into the bouillon and, as soon as it starts
to bubble, switch off the heat and pour the bouillon
over the meat and vegetables. Serve immediately.

sweet couscous with raisins and onions
serves 6 · preparation 20 minutes · cooking 30 minutes

4 onions
3/4 cup (185 mL) butter, two-thirds for the meat,
    one-third for the couscous
2 Tbsp (30 mL) olive oil
1 large, farm-raised chicken, weighing about 4 lb (1.8 kg),
    cut into pieces
1 cinnamon stick
1/2 tsp (2 mL) ground ginger
1/2 tsp (2 mL) turmeric
pinch of saffron
1/2 tsp (2 mL) pepper
1 Tbsp (15 mL) salt
4 cups (1 L) raisins
2 Tbsp (30 mL) superfine sugar
2 Tbsp (30 mL) honey
1 Tbsp (15 mL) cinnamon
3 cups (750 mL) medium-grain couscous

Peel and finely chop the onions. Heat two-thirds
of the butter and the oil in a couscous steamer
and soften the onions. Add the chicken pieces, the
cinnamon stick, spices, and salt. Pour in enough
water to cover and let cook for 20 minutes.

Remove the onions with a slotted spoon. Put
2 ladlefuls of the bouillon in a small saucepan
with the raisins, sugar, honey, and cinnamon.
Let simmer for 5 minutes.

Meanwhile prepare the couscous following the
method on page 109.

Arrange the chicken pieces in a serving dish,
surround with the couscous, and top with the
spicy raisins.

sweet and salty couscous "medfoun"
serves 6 • preparation 20 minutes • cooking 25 minutes

2 onions
1/3 cup (80 mL) butter, half for the meat, half for
   the couscous
2 Tbsp (30 mL) sunflower oil
2 small chicken (2 young rooster), cut into pieces
1 bunch of cilantro
1/4 tsp (1 mL) ground ginger
1/2 tsp (2 mL) turmeric
pinch of saffron
1/4 tsp (1 mL) pepper
1/3 cup + 4 tsp (100 mL) water
3 cups (750 mL) medium-grain couscous
salt
1 Tbsp (15 mL) cinnamon to garnish
superfine or confectioners' sugar to serve

Peel and finely chop the onions. Melt half the
butter and the oil in a heavy-based pot and soften
the onion for 2 minutes.

Add the chicken pieces with the chopped cilantro,
spices, salt to taste, and water. Cook for 20 minutes,
stirring from time to time. When the meat is
tender, remove the casserole from the heat,
strip the meat from the bones, and mix well with
the sauce.

Meanwhile prepare the couscous following the
method on page 109, replacing the bouillon with
boiling salted water.

Place a third of the couscous on a large serving
dish. Spread with half the chicken mixture then
cover with another third of the couscous. Spread
with the remaining chicken mixture and top
with the remaining couscous. Garnish with the
cinnamon and serve with the sugar.

couscous with lben
serves 6 • preparation 5 minutes • cooking 10 minutes

3 cups (750 mL) medium-grain couscous
2 1/2 cups (625 mL) frozen fava beans
8 cups (2 L) "Lben" milk or "lait battu" (Moroccan
   fermented milk–substitute with buttermilk)
pinch of salt

Prepare the couscous following the method on
page 109, replacing the bouillon with boiling salted
water. Meanwhile, cook the fava beans in boiling
salted water for 10 minutes.

Separate the couscous grains with your hands
then fill bowls half full with the couscous and
sprinkle with the milk. Serve the fava beans
separately.

This couscous can also be served with 1 Tbsp
(15 mL) sugar in each bowl, according to taste,
and eaten as a dessert.

couscous with cinnamon and milk
serves 6 • preparation 5 minutes • cooking 10 minutes

3 cups (750 mL) fine-grain couscous
3/4 cup (185 mL) butter
1 Tbsp (15 mL) cinnamon to garnish
1 Tbsp (15 mL) superfine sugar + extra to serve
4 cups (1 L) milk to accompany

Prepare the couscous following the method on
page 109, but incorporating the 3/4 cup (5 oz/
150 g) butter.

Present on a serving dish in a cone shape,
garnished with the cinnamon and sugar. Serve with
extra sugar to taste and the milk to accompany.

TIP: This couscous is generally served as a light
evening meal, accompanied with milk. You can
soak 2/3 cup (160 mL) raisins and stir them through
the couscous.

pastillas

bread

To a Moroccan, bread (*khobz*) is sacred and must never be squandered. In rural areas it is called *kesra*. All that is required is some flour (white or whole wheat), a little water, sugar and salt, a little yeast, and a light working (for the dough must not rise too much), then the loaves rest wrapped in cloth before being placed on a large baking sheet. The bread is shaped into flat rounds and has only one rising. Aniseed or sesame seed is often worked into the dough or sprinkled on the light crust. The soft interior is fairly light to absorb the sauce of a tagine but must be sufficiently dense to carry other food to the mouth: in Morocco food is traditionally eaten without cutlery. Food is eaten with the thumb, index, and middle finger of one hand, with the aid of a piece of bread. Flatter loaves serve to sandwich kabob meat.

how to make pastilla

utter a round baking pan or pie
te.

2 Lay 2 sheets of oiled and buttered
warka or phyllo pastry on top.

3 With your fingers coated with a light
mixture of flour and water, stick 4 more
sheets of pastry around the rim,
leaving most of each sheet off the pan
in the way that petals are arranged
around the center of a flower.

y another warka or phyllo sheet
he baking pan and butter well.

5 Spread a layer of filling over the
base.

6 Arrange the other ingredients
evenly.

over with another sheet of pastry.

8 Fold in the "petals," sticking each
one to the others with the flour and
water mix.

9 Finish with a final sheet of pastry,
sticking it around the edges. Butter
the surface well.

pastillas

chicken pastilla
serves 8 · preparation 30 minutes · cooking 45 minutes

3 lb (1.5 kg) onions
2 bunches of flat-leaf parsley
1 cup (250 mL) butter
2 Tbsp (30 mL) sunflower oil
1 large chicken, weighing about 4 lb (1.8 kg), cut into 8 pieces
$1/2$ tsp (2 mL) turmeric
pinch of saffron
$1/2$ tsp (2 mL) salt
$1/2$ tsp (2 mL) pepper
12 eggs
1 lemon
1 pack of warka or phyllo pastry

TO SEAL
3 Tbsp (45 mL) all-purpose flour
2 Tbsp (30 mL) water

Peel and finely mince the onions with the parsley. Heat the butter and oil in a heavy-based pot and cook the onions, parsley, chicken pieces, spices, and half the salt and pepper. When the chicken is cooked, remove the skin and bones and reserve the meat.

Beat the eggs with the remaining salt and pepper and pour into the cooking juices that remain in the pot. Stir rapidly with a wooden spatula to prevent them sticking and cook until they set. Transfer to a plate and let cool. Squeeze over the lemon juice.

Preheat the oven to 350°F (180°C/Gas 4).

Prepare the pastilla following the steps on page 123. Spread the cooled eggs in a thick layer over the base and place the chicken meat on top. Cover with the warka or phyllo sheets, seal, and butter as described.

Transfer to the oven and bake for 30 minutes. Serve hot.

pastillas

pigeon pastilla
serves 8 · preparation 40 minutes · cooking 45 minutes

3 large onions
2 bunches of flat-leaf parsley
$1/2$ bunch of cilantro
$3/4$ cup + 1 Tbsp (200 mL) butter
$2^1/2$ Tbsp (37.5 mL) sunflower oil
7 pigeons, cut into quarters
$1/2$ tsp (2 mL) salt
$1/2$ tsp (2 mL) pepper
1 tsp (5 mL) cinnamon
$3/4$ cup + 1 Tbsp (200 mL) water
12 eggs
pinch of saffron
$1/4$ tsp (1 mL) turmeric
$1^1/2$ cups (375 mL) skinned almonds
$1/2$ cup (125 mL) superfine sugar
1 pack of warka or phyllo pastry

TO SEAL
3 Tbsp (45 mL) all-purpose flour
2 Tbsp (30 mL) water

TO GARNISH
$3/4$ cup + 1 Tbsp (100 mL) confectioners' sugar
1 Tbsp (15 mL) cinnamon

Peel and finely mince the onions with the herbs. Heat the butter and sunflower oil in a heavy-based pot and add the pigeon, onions and herbs, salt, pepper, and half the cinnamon. Mix well, pour in the water, and cover with the lid. After about 15 minutes, when the pigeon is cooked, transfer the pieces to a plate and remove the white meat from the bones (keep the thighs whole).

Beat the eggs with a little salt and pepper, the saffron, and the turmeric and pour into the cooking juices that remain in the casserole. Stir rapidly with a wooden spatula to prevent them sticking and cook until they set. Transfer to a plate and let cool.

Dry-fry the almonds in a skillet then set aside to cool. Once they are cool, crush and mix with the sugar and the remaining cinnamon and set aside.

Preheat the oven to 350°F (180°C/Gas 4).

Prepare the pastilla following the steps on page 123. Spread the cooled eggs in a thick layer over the base and place the pigeon meat on top. Generously sprinkle with the almond, sugar, and cinnamon mixture. Cover with the warka or phyllo sheets, seal, and butter as described.

Transfer to the oven and bake for 30 minutes.

To serve, sprinkle the surface of the pastilla with the confectioners' sugar and use the cinnamon to form intersecting lines.

pastillas

fish and shrimp pastilla
serves 8 · preparation 15 minutes · marinating 1 hour · cooking 45 minutes

2 lb (1 kg) white fish fillets
1 lb (500 g) raw shrimp, shelled
1 bunch of cilantro
1 bunch of flat-leaf parsley
3 garlic cloves
1 Tbsp (15 mL) paprika
pinch of cayenne pepper
1/2 tsp (2 mL) cumin
pinch of mace
1/4 tsp (1 mL) salt
1/4 tsp (1 mL) pepper
2 Tbsp (30 mL) vinegar
1/4 cup (60 mL) butter
2 Tbsp (30 mL) olive oil
1 large bowl of fine Chinese noodles, soaked
1 pack of warka or phyllo pastry

TO SEAL
3 Tbsp (45 mL) all-purpose flour
2 Tbsp (30 mL) water

Put the fish and shrimp in a large bowl with the washed and chopped herbs, the finely minced garlic, all the spices, the salt and pepper, and the vinegar. Cover with plastic wrap and refrigerate for 1 hour.

Melt the butter in a heavy-based pot, add the oil, and cook the fish and shrimp until the flesh begins to flake apart. Stir in the soaked noodles and cook for 10 minutes over low heat.

Preheat the oven to 350°F (180°C/Gas 4).

Prepare the pastilla following the steps on page 123. Spread the filling in a thick layer over the base. Cover with the warka or phyllo sheets, seal, and butter as described.

Transfer to the oven and bake for 30 minutes.

pastillas

pastilla with custard
serves 8 • preparation 30 minutes • cooking 20 minutes

1 1/2 cups (310 mL) skinned almonds
1/4 cup (50 mL) superfine sugar
20 sheets of warka or phyllo pastry
sunflower oil for frying

FOR THE CUSTARD
4 egg yolks
2/3 cup (160 mL) superfine sugar
1 Tbsp (15 mL) vanilla sugar
2 Tbsp (30 mL) all-purpose flour
3 cups (750 mL) boiling milk

TO DECORATE
4 egg whites
1/4 cup (60 mL) superfine sugar
1/2 cup (125 mL) superfine sugar for the caramel

First dry-toast the almonds then set aside to cool. When they are cold, roughly chop and add the superfine sugar.

Prepare the custard. Put the egg yolks in a saucepan with the sugars and beat to dissolve. Incorporate the flour then pour in the boiling milk, beating vigorously over low heat until the custard thickens. Let cool completely.

Whip the egg whites with the 1/4 cup (60 mL) superfine sugar until stiff. Cook spoonfuls of the meringue mixture in boiling water and set aide.

One hour before serving, fold the warka or phyllo pastry in four, fan fashion, and fry them, a few at a time, then drain on paper towels.

Place four of the pastry fans on a round plate to reassemble a circle, then add a second layer. Spread with half of the cold custard and sprinkle over a third of the almonds. Repeat with two layers of pastry fans, the remaining custard, and another third of the almonds. Top with the remaining four fans.

Decorate with the meringue and sprinkle over the remaining almonds. Quickly prepare a caramel with the 1/2 cup (125 mL) of superfine sugar and 1 Tbsp (15 mL) of water. Pour over the pastilla and serve immediately.

desserts and sweet things

fruits

In all Moroccan homes, meals end with fresh fruit. During celebratory meals, beautifully arranged fruit—piled on platters or sometimes on a bed of ice—is served in praise of the season. If fruit is prepared, it is scented with orange-flower water, dusted with cinnamon, or strewn with crushed nuts. Indeed, nothing is more refreshing at the end of a meal than a simple salad of oranges or a pomegranate with a sprinkling of orange-flower water and a light dusting of confectioners' sugar. Shredded carrot can be served in the same way.

pastries

Moroccans end a meal more readily with fruit than a sweet pastry. Traditional desserts are fairly unusual, but something sweet between courses, milk rice pudding for example, is extremely popular. Moroccan pastries are similar to those of the Middle East but very different in appearance. Almonds reign supreme, especially finely ground. Confectioners' sugar, cinnamon, orange-flower water, rose water, and honey are much favored. Nuts, dates, dried figs, sesame seeds, and, to a lesser degree, pistachio nuts play a role in the art of the pastry chef. And if these delicious morsels rarely round off a meal, they are the preferred accompaniment to mint tea, the drink seen everywhere in Morocco, which is offered as a gesture of welcome.

desserts and sweet things

squash or pumpkin preserve
preparation 15 minutes · cooking 20 minutes

2 lb (1 kg) red squash or pumpkin
3 cups (750 mL) superfine sugar
1 lemon
1 Tbsp (15 mL) cinnamon

Peel the squash, remove the seeds and fiber, and dice the flesh very small. Drop into boiling water and cook for 5 minutes.

Drain the squash and tip into a large saucepan, sprinkle over the sugar, and squeeze in the lemon juice. Cook over a low heat for 15 minutes, gently stirring from time to time. Stir in the cinnamon at the end of cooking.

eggplant preserve
soaking 12 hours · preparation 10 minutes cooking 45 minutes

2 lb (1 kg) very small eggplants
2 lb (1 kg) granulated sugar
3/4 cup + 1 Tbsp (200 mL) water
1 lemon
5 or 6 cloves
1/4 tsp (1 mL) quatre épices (a blend of ground white
    pepper, nutmeg, cloves, and cinnamon)
2 small pieces gum arabic
salt

Prick the eggplants all over with a fork. Place them one by one in a large bowl of salted water and leave to soak overnight.

The following day, rinse the eggplants in plenty of running water, then drop into boiling water and cook for 10 minutes. Drain and set aside.

Put the sugar into a large saucepan with the water and allow to slowly dissolve. Squeeze in the lemon juice, then add the spices, the gum arabic, and the drained eggplants. Once the eggplants have absorbed the sugar, turn off the heat and drain.

candied oranges
soaking 12 hours · preparation 20 minutes · cooking 20 minutes

3 lb (1.5 kg) Navel oranges
2 lb (1 kg) superfine sugar
1 lemon
1/4 tsp (1 mL) salt

Select thick-skinned oranges. Grate them to remove the zest then place the oranges in a bowl of salted water and leave to soak overnight.

The following day, rinse the oranges in plenty of running water, then bring to a boil in a saucepan of water. As soon as the water boils, remove and drain the oranges. Cut into quarters or sixths, depending on size. Place the pieces in a preserving pan, cover with sugar, squeeze in the lemon juice and cook over a low heat, gently turning the pieces once to avoid damaging them.

Once the oranges are a rich golden color and the syrup has reduced, remove from the heat and arrange in serving dishes.

raisin and walnut preserve "mrozia"
makes about 30 · preparation 5 minutes · cooking 50 minutes

2 lb (1 kg) large golden raisins
3/4 cup + 1 Tbsp (200 mL) superfine sugar
1/4 tsp (1 mL) cinnamon
2 Tbsp (30 mL) peanut oil
3/4 cup + 1 Tbsp (200 mL) water
4 cups (1 L) shelled walnuts

Wash the raisins and place in a large saucepan with the sugar, cinnamon, oil, and water. Cook over very low heat for about 45 minutes, stirring from time to time; the raisins should not be too colored.

Meanwhile, dry-toast the walnuts over low heat for 5 minutes then remove and let cool. When they are cold, roughly crush them in your hand and add them to the raisins 5 minutes before the end of cooking. Tip into a preserves jar and let cool.

desserts and sweet things

preserved clementines
makes about 15 · Soaking 12 hours · preparation 10 minutes · cooking 2 hours

2 lb (1 kg) small clementines
2 lb (1 kg) sugar
1 lemon
4 cups (1 L) water

Place the clementines in a bowl of water and leave to soak overnight.

Using a kabob skewer, pierce the fruit from top to bottom and on the sides.

Place the clementines in a large saucepan, sprinkle with sugar, squeeze in the lemon juice, and pour in the water. Let the sugar dissolve over low heat.

Cook for a total of 2 hours, in three or four stages, letting the fruit cool between each stage.

desserts and sweet things

caramelized sesame seeds
makes 20 · preparation 10 minutes · cooking 10 minutes

1 glass of white sesame seeds
1 glass of superfine sugar
1 Tbsp (15 mL) peanut oil

Whatever quantity of caramelized sesame seeds you wish to make, keep the proportions of sesame seed and sugar the same.

Heat a nonstick skillet over very low heat. Add the sesame seeds and sugar and let the sugar melt. Let it brown until it turns to caramel.

Oil a metal tray or baking pan and tip the mixture in. Roll out using a rolling pin. While the mixture is still hot and soft, cut into small pieces using a knife.

caramelized almonds
makes about 20 · preparation 10 minutes · cooking 15 minutes

1 glass raw, unskinned almonds
1/2 glass superfine sugar
1 Tbsp (15 mL) peanut oil

Whatever quantity of caramelized almonds you wish to make, keep the proportions of almonds and sugar the same.

Heat a nonstick skillet over very low heat. Add the almonds and sugar and let the sugar melt, stirring from time to time with a wooden spatula until the sugar turns to caramel.

Oil a metal tray or baking pan, then use a spoon to remove a few almonds and form into a small pile on the tray. Repeat with all the almonds.

Once the almonds are cold, transfer from the tray to a serving plate.

desserts and sweet things

almond "ghoriba" (cookies)
makes about 30 · preparation 20 minutes · baking 20 minutes

2 lb (1 kg) skinned almonds, + a few extra to decorate
4 1/2 cups (1.1 L) confectioners' sugar
1/2 Tbsp (7.5 mL) baking powder
3 Tbsp (45 mL) melted butter
6 egg yolks
2 whole eggs
rind of 1 lemon
2/3 cup (160 mL) orange-flower water

Preheat the oven to 350°F (180°C/Gas 4).

Finely chop the almonds in a blender.

Tip the almonds into a mixing bowl and mix in two-thirds of the confectioners' sugar, the baking powder, butter, egg yolks and whole eggs, and the lemon rind.

Add the orange-flower water to make a dough and, with wetted hands, form into balls about the size of a walnut.

Tip the remaining confectioners' sugar onto a plate and roll each ball in it until coated. Place on an oiled baking sheet, spaced well apart. Poke an almond into the top of each one and transfer to the oven. Bake for 15 minutes.

date crescents
makes about 40 · preparation 30 minutes · baking 15 minutes

FOR THE PASTRY
4 1/2 cups (1.1 L) all-purpose flour
pinch of baking powder
1/2 cup (125 mL) granulated sugar
1 cup (250 mL) butter

FOR THE FILLING
8 oz (250 g) date paste (or use stoned chopped dates)
1 knob of butter
1/2 tsp (2 mL) cinnamon

1 cup (250 mL) confectioners' sugar

Preheat the oven to 300°F (150°C/Gas 2).

Make the pastry by mixing all the ingredients to form a dough. Let it rest while you make the filling.

Mix all the ingredients for the filling and form into balls the size of a hazelnut.

Now take the pastry and make into balls the size of a walnut. Press a ball of filling into each one, close the pastry around it, then form it into the shape of a crescent. Place on an oiled baking sheet.

Bake for 15 minutes. Remove from the oven and pass each crescent through the confectioners' sugar to coat on all sides.

little "mhancha" (Moroccan snakes)
makes about 10 · preparation 30 minutes · baking 15 minutes

FOR THE FILLING
3 cups (750 mL) skinned almonds, + 10 extra to decorate
1 1/4 cups (310 mL) superfine sugar
5 Tbsp (75 mL) orange-flower water
1 Tbsp (15 mL) cinnamon
3/4 cup (185 mL) butter, melted

10 sheets of warka or phyllo pastry
1 beaten egg
1/3 cup (80 mL) butter, melted
2/3 cup (160 mL) honey

Chop the almonds in a blender, then add the sugar and 1 Tbsp (15 mL) orange-flower water and chop again until fine.

Tip the mixture into a bowl and add the cinnamon and butter. Mix to a dough and form into rolls 6 inches (15 cm) long and 1 inch (2 cm) wide. Set aside.

Preheat the oven to 250°F (120°C/Gas 1/2).

Cut a sheet of warka or phyllo pastry in two, place with the two straight edges facing you, fold them over by 1 inch (2 cm), and stick them with the beaten egg.

Place an almond roll on the rounded edge and roll up in the warka or phyllo, then roll the length into a spiral. Repeat with the remaining pastry sheets and rolls of filling. Place on an oiled baking sheet and brush with the melted butter. Press a whole almond into the center of each spiral.

Transfer to the oven and bake for 12-15 minutes. Meanwhile, heat the honey and remaining orange-flower water together.

When the cakes are cooked, dip them, still hot, in the honey mixture and arrange on a serving platter.

desserts and sweet things

gazelle horns
makes 50 • preparation 25 minutes • baking 15 minutes

FOR THE PASTRY
2³/4 cups (685 mL) cake flour
¹/4 cup (60 mL) softened butter
¹/4 cup (60 mL) orange-flower water
¹/4 cup (60 mL) confectioners' sugar

FOR THE FILLING
3 cups (750 mL) skinned almonds
1¹/4 cups (310 mL) superfine sugar
1 Tbsp (15 mL) orange-flower water
2 Tbsp (30 mL) butter, melted
1 Tbsp (15 mL) cinnamon

Rub together the ingredients for the pastry. If it seems too dry, add a little water or extra orange-flower water. Let it rest in the refrigerator while you prepare the filling.

Chop the almonds once in a blender then add the sugar and orange-flower water and chop again until fine. Tip the mixture into a bowl and add the cinnamon and butter. Mix to a dough and form into sticks 3 inches (8 cm) long.

Preheat the oven to 350°F (180°C/Gas 4).

Divide the pastry into about 50 small balls. Roll out the balls into thin rectangles and place a stick of almond paste on each one. Close the pastry around the filling, press to seal and trim to form a horn shape. Place them on an oiled baking sheet.

Transfer to the oven and bake for 15 minutes, then let cool before serving.

VARIATION

You can also make gazelle horns covered in confectioners' sugar. Follow the method above but make the dough a little thicker. Pour 6 Tbsp (90 mL) orange-flower water in a shallow dish and about 1 cup (250 mL) of confectioners' sugar on a plate. Dip the cooked gazelle horns, still hot, in the orange-flower water then pass through the confectioners' sugar to coat on all sides. Place on a wire rack to dry.

pistachio baklavas
makes 24 • preparation 30 minutes • resting 12 hours • baking 20 minutes

2 cups (500 mL) raw pistachio nuts
³/4 cup + 1 Tbsp (100 g) sugar
1 Tbsp (15 mL) orange-flower water
8 sheets of warka or phyllo pastry
1 egg white
¹/2 cup (125 mL) butter

FOR THE GLAZE
¹/2 cup (125 mL) honey
2 Tbsp (30 mL) orange-flower water

Dry-roast the pistachio nuts in a medium-hot oven for 15 minutes then rub off the skins and finely chop with the sugar. Add the orange-flower water then set aside the mixture.

Take 2 warka or phyllo pastry sheets, overlap them slightly on the long sides, and stick them together with egg white. Butter generously then fold in the rounded top and bottom edges to form a rectangle. Place a quarter of the filling in the center. Fold over the pastry sheet once into the center then a second time to bring in the sides, flattening slightly to make a parcel about 2 inches (5 cm) wide. Repeat to make a total of four long parcels.

Put the cakes on a tray, cover with plastic wrap, and place a weight on top. Leave overnight.

The following day, preheat the oven to 300°F (150°F/Gas 2).

Unwrap the cakes and place them in a buttered baking pan or ovenproof dish. Slice each cake into six pieces, on the diagonal using a very sharp knife. Do not separate them completely.

Transfer the pan to the oven and bake for 20 minutes. Meanwhile heat the honey with the orange-flower water for the glaze. Immediately the baklavas are cooked, coat them with the hot glaze. Let stand for 1 hour before removing them from the pan to a serving platter.

desserts and sweet things

moroccan rice pudding
serves 6 · preparation 5 minutes · cooking 40 minutes

1¹/₂ cups (375 mL) rice
1 knob of butter
8 cups (2 L) milk
³/₄ cup + 1 Tbsp (200 mL) superfine sugar
¹/₂ tsp (2 mL) salt
1 Tbsp (15 mL) orange-flower water

Cook the rice following the packet instructions. Once the water has been completely absorbed, add the butter, milk, sugar, and salt. Bring back to a boil, stirring from time to time so that the rice does not stick, add the orange-flower water, and continue to stir.

When the milk has the consistency of custard, remove from the heat and continue to stir to prevent a skin from forming. Serve in a large bowl.

desserts and sweet things

honey halva "griwach"
makes 20 · preparation 30 minutes · cooking 15 minutes

1 glass of white sesame seeds
9 cups (2.25 mL) cake flour
1 package active dry yeast
4 tsp baking powder
1/2 tsp (2 mL) turmeric
pinch of saffron
1 glass of a mixture of melted butter and sunflower oil
3 Tbsp (45 mL) vinegar
oil for deep-frying

FOR THE GLAZE
1 1/2 cups (375 mL) runny honey
2/3 cup (160 mL) orange-flower water

Dry-roast the sesame seeds in a skillet over low heat. Remove and let cool.

Tip the flour into a large bowl and add in all the other ingredients. Work the dough thoroughly as if making bread. Roll it out and cut into 4 inch x 1 inch (10 cm x 8 cm) rectangles, about 1 inch (3 cm) thick. Twist the rectangles and join the two ends. Heat the oil in a deep-fat fryer or deep-sided skillet and fry the cakes in batches until golden on all sides.

Meanwhile heat the honey with the orange-flower water and dip the hot halva first in the glaze and then in the sesame seeds. Let cool before serving.

desserts and sweet things

"m'semen" (Moroccan pancakes)
makes 15–20 · preparation 20 minutes · resting 20 minutes · cooking 20 minutes

4^1/$_2$ cups (1.1 L) bread flour
1^1/$_4$ cups (310 mL) cream of wheat
^{1}/$_2$ package active dry yeast
^{1}/$_2$ tsp (2 mL) salt
^{3}/$_4$ cup + 1 Tbsp (200 mL) tepid water
5 Tbsp (75 mL) peanut oil
^{1}/$_2$ cup (125 mL) butter

Mix together all the dry ingredients in a large bowl and add the water little by little, working it in until you have a very supple dough. Let rest for 5 minutes.

Divide the dough into pieces the size of a tennis ball and place them on an oiled countertop. Let rest for an additional 5 minutes.

Melt the butter and mix with the oil. Coat your hands in the mixture and, taking each ball in turn, stretch the dough into a large, very thin, almost transparent, disk.

Coat your hands again in the butter and oil mixture, fold the disks in three, then into three again to form a square, tuck in the ends, and let rest for 10 minutes.

Cook each parcel in a hot skillet for 1 minute, turning over halfway through. Serve hot, with either sugar or honey.

indexes

recipe list

acknowledgments

A big thank you to Jacques Cohen, who was kind enough to welcome us into his house in Essaouira for the photography. This book owes much to his hospitality.

Thanks to Maki, in Essaouira, to have so kindly loaned us the beautiful items from his shop.

props by Stéphanie Huré

Library and Achives Canada Cataloguing in Publication
Bénady, Ghislaine
Morocco / Ghislaine Bénady and Najat Sefrioui; photography by Michel Reuss.
ISBN: 978-1-55285-968-1
1. Cookery, Moroccan. I. Sefrioui, Najat II. Reuss, Michel III. Title
TX725.M8B44 2009   641.5964   C2009-902684-8

Printed in China

09 10 11 12 13   5 4 3 2 1